HEALTH CARE IN TRANSITION

CONNECTED HEALTH CARE

A ROADMAP FOR INTEROPERABLE HEALTH INFORMATION AND TECHNOLOGY

HEALTH CARE IN TRANSITION

Additional books in this series can be found on Nova's website under the Series tab.

Additional e-books in this series can be found on Nova's website under the eBooks tab.

HEALTH CARE IN TRANSITION

CONNECTED HEALTH CARE

A ROADMAP FOR INTEROPERABLE HEALTH INFORMATION AND TECHNOLOGY

ELAINE RAMIREZ
EDITOR

New York

NOTICE TO THE READER

The Publisher has taken reasonable care in the preparation of this book, but makes no expressed or implied warranty of any kind and assumes no responsibility for any errors or omissions. No liability is assumed for incidental or consequential damages in connection with or arising out of information contained in this book. The Publisher shall not be liable for any special, consequential, or exemplary damages resulting, in whole or in part, from the readers' use of, or reliance upon, this material. Any parts of this book based on government reports are so indicated and copyright is claimed for those parts to the extent applicable to compilations of such works.

Independent verification should be sought for any data, advice or recommendations contained in this book. In addition, no responsibility is assumed by the publisher for any injury and/or damage to persons or property arising from any methods, products, instructions, ideas or otherwise contained in this publication.

This publication is designed to provide accurate and authoritative information with regard to the subject matter covered herein. It is sold with the clear understanding that the Publisher is not engaged in rendering legal or any other professional services. If legal or any other expert assistance is required, the services of a competent person should be sought. FROM A DECLARATION OF PARTICIPANTS JOINTLY ADOPTED BY A COMMITTEE OF THE AMERICAN BAR ASSOCIATION AND A COMMITTEE OF PUBLISHERS.

Additional color graphics may be available in the e-book version of this book.

Library of Congress Cataloging-in-Publication Data

ISBN: 978-1-63484-947-0

Published by Nova Science Publishers, Inc. † New York

CONTENTS

PREFACE

The U.S. Department of Health and Human Services (HHS) has a critical responsibility to advance the connectivity of electronic health information and interoperability of health information technology (health IT). This is consistent with its mission to protect the health of all Americans and provide essential human services, especially for those who are least able to help themselves. This work has become particularly urgent with the need to address the national priority of better and more affordable health care, leading to better population health. Achieving this goal will only be possible with a strong, flexible health IT ecosystem that can appropriately support transparency and decision-making, reduce redundancy, inform payment reform, and help to transform care into a model that enhances access and truly addresses health beyond the confines of the health care system. Such an infrastructure will support more efficient and effective systems, scientific advancement, and lead to a continuously improving health system that empowers individuals, customizes treatment, and accelerates cure of disease. This book's purpose is to better inform decision making to improve individual health, community health, and population health. It also describes the policy and technical actions needed to realize the vision of a seamless data system.

In: Connected Health Care
Editor: Elaine Ramirez

ISBN: 978-1-63484-947-0

Chapter 1

CONNECTING HEALTH AND CARE FOR THE NATION: A 10 YEAR VISION TO ACHIEVE AN INTEROPERABLE HEALTH IT INFRASTRUCTURE*

Office of the National Coordinator for Health Information Technology

OVERVIEW

The U.S. Department of Health and Human Services (HHS) has a critical responsibility to advance the connectivity of electronic health information and interoperability of health information technology (health IT). This is consistent with its mission to protect the health of all Americans and provide essential human services, especially for those who are least able to help themselves. This work has become particularly urgent with the need to address the national priority of better and more affordable health care, leading to better population health. Achieving this goal will only be possible with a strong, flexible health IT ecosystem that can appropriately support transparency and decision-making, reduce redundancy, inform payment reform, and help to transform care into a model that enhances access and truly addresses health beyond the

* This is an edited, reformatted and augmented version of document issued by the Office of the National Coordinator for Health Information Technology, 2014.

confines of the health care system. Such an infrastructure will support more efficient and effective systems, scientific advancement, and lead to a continuously improving health system that empowers individuals, customizes treatment, and accelerates cure of disease.

In the past decade, there has been dramatic progress in building the foundation of a health IT infrastructure across the country that is resilient and flexible to accommodate many types of change. Through deliberate policy and programmatic action, the majority of meaningful use[1] eligible hospitals and professionals have adopted and are meaningfully using health IT. This progress has laid a strong base upon which we can build. However, there is much work to do to see that every individual and their care providers can get the health information they need in an electronic format when and how they need it to make care convenient and well-coordinated and allow for improvements in overall health. There is no better time than now to renew our focus on a nationwide, interoperable health IT infrastructure – one in which all individuals, their families, and their health care providers have appropriate access to health information that facilitates informed decision-making, supports coordinated health management, allows patients to be active partners in their health and care, and improves the overall health of our population. This is not just a technology challenge.

Broad adoption of health IT will require that health information can be easily and appropriately shared to support multiple uses. For instance, the national priority of cost-effective care requires information about quality and use of services to be available to consumers, providers, payers, and employers. Further, physicians expect health IT to enable and support patient care. And finally, there is mounting interest by consumers and innovators in creating meaningful opportunities for individuals to partner in their own health care.

New technology and market changes have opened the door to creating a more integrated and flexible environment that will not only serve us better in the present day, but will allow for ongoing innovation in the future. This paper is an invitation to health IT stakeholders – clinicians, hospitals, public health, technology developers, payers, researchers, policymakers, individuals, and many others – to join ONC in figuring out how we can collectively achieve interoperability across the health IT ecosystem (Figure 1).

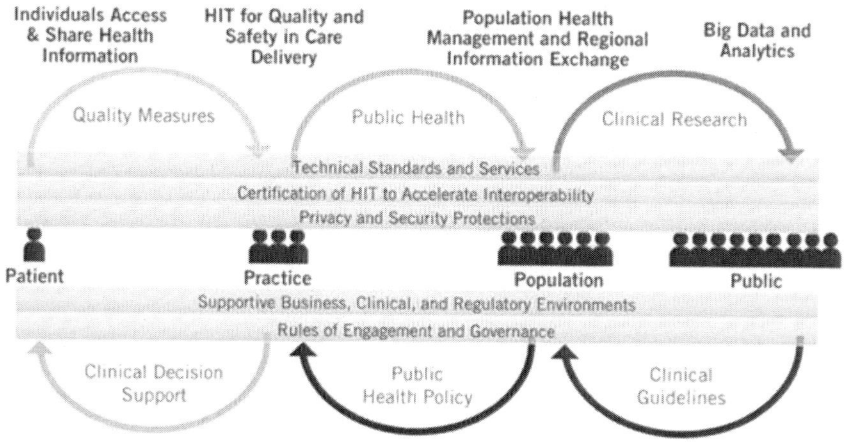

Figure 1. Health IT Ecosystem.

VISION FOR THE FUTURE

An interoperable health IT ecosystem makes the right data available to the right people at the right time across products and organizations in a way that can be relied upon and meaningfully used by recipients. By 2024, individuals, care providers, communities, and researchers should have an array of interoperable health IT products and services that allow the health care system to continuously learn and advance the goal of improved health care. This "learning health system" should also enable lower health care costs, improved population health, truly empower consumers, and drive innovation. For example, all individuals, their families, and care providers should be able to send, receive, find, and use health information in a manner that is appropriate, secure, timely, and reliable.[2]

Individuals should be able to securely share electronic health information with care providers and make use of the information to support their own health and wellness through informed shared decision-making. An interoperable health IT ecosystem should support critical public health functions such as real-time disease surveillance and disaster response, and data aggregation for research and value-based payment that rewards higher *quality* care, not necessarily a higher *quantity* of care.

CONTEXT

The nation has made dramatic advancements in digitizing the care delivery system during the past decade:

- Over one-half of office-based professionals and more than 8 in 10 hospitals are meaningfully using electronic health records (EHRs), which will require them to electronically exchange standardized patient information to support safe care transitions (Figure 2).[3]
- One-half of hospitals are able to electronically search for patient information from sources beyond their organization or health system (Figure 3).[4]
- All 50 states have some form of health information exchange services available to support care.[5]
- Through the Blue Button Initiative, more than half of individual consumers and patients are able to access at least some of their own health information electronically via the combined contributions of providers, health plans, pharmacies, and labs.[6] Technological innovations such as wearable devices, remote sensing devices, and telehealth support at-home and virtual care models and new roles for patients.

Figure 2. Hospitals and Professionals That Have Demonstrated Meaningful Use of Certified EHR Technology 2014.

Figure 3. U.S. Hospitals' Capability to Electronically Query Patient Health Information from Outside Their Organization or System 2013.

This significant progress has created a growing demand for interoperability that not only supports the care continuum, but supports health generally. Electronic health information needs to be available for appropriate use in solving major challenges such as providing more effective care and informing and accelerating scientific research. Despite significant progress in establishing standards and services to support health information exchange and interoperability, it is not the norm that electronic health information is shared beyond groups of health care providers who subscribe to specific services or organizations. This frequently means that patients' electronic health information is not shared across organizational, vendor and geographic boundaries. Electronic health information is also not sufficiently standardized to allow seamless interoperability, as it is still inconsistently expressed with vocabulary, structure, and format, thereby limiting the potential uses of the information to improve health and care. We must learn from the important lessons and local successes[7] of previous and current health information exchange infrastructure to improve interoperability in support of nationwide exchange and use of health information across the public and private sector.

Guiding Principles

As we work toward this vision for the future interoperable health IT ecosystem, we will plan and execute our work to align with a set of guiding principles:

- Build upon the existing health IT infrastructure. Significant investments have been made in health IT across the care delivery system and in other relevant sectors that need to exchange information with individuals and care providers. To the extent possible, we will encourage stakeholders to build from existing health IT infrastructure, increasing interoperability and functionality as needed.
- One size does not fit all. Interoperability requires technical and policy conformance among networks, technical systems and their components. It also requires behavior and culture change on the part of users. We will strive for baseline interoperability across health IT infrastructure, while allowing innovators and technologists to vary the user experience (the feel and function of tools) in order to best meet the user's needs based on the scenario at hand, technology available, workflow design, personal preferences, and other factors.
- Empower individuals. Members of the public are rapidly adopting technology to manage numerous aspects of their lives, including health and wellness. However, many of these tools do not yet integrate information from the health care delivery system. Health information from the care delivery system should be easily accessible to individuals and empower them to become more active partners in their health just as other kinds of data are empowering them in other aspects of their lives.
- Leverage the market. Demand for interoperability from health IT users is a powerful driver to advance our vision. As payment and care delivery reform increase demand for interoperability, we will work with and support these efforts.
- Simplify. Where possible, simpler solutions should be implemented first, with allowance for more complex methods in the future.
- Maintain modularity. Complex systems are more resilient to change when they are divided into independent components that can be connected together. Because medicine and technology will change over time, we must preserve systems' abilities to evolve and take

advantage of the best of technology and health care delivery. Modularity creates flexibility that allows innovation and adoption of new, more efficient approaches over time without overhauling entire systems.

- Consider the current environment and support multiple levels of advancement. Not every clinical practice will incorporate health information technology into their work in the next 3-10 years, and not every practice will adopt health IT at the same level of sophistication. We must therefore account for a range of capabilities among information sources and information users, including EHR and non-EHR users, as we advance interoperability. Individuals and caregivers have an ongoing need to find, send, receive, and use their own health information both within and outside the care delivery system and interoperable infrastructure should enable this.
- Focus on value. We will strive to make sure our interoperability efforts yield the greatest value to individuals and care providers; improved health, health care, and lower costs should be measurable over time and at a minimum, offset the resource investment.
- Protect privacy and security in all aspects of interoperability. It is essential to maintain public trust that health information is safe and secure. To better establish and maintain that trust, we will strive to ensure that appropriate, strong, and effective safeguards for health information are in place as interoperability increases across the industry. We will also support greater transparency for individuals regarding the business practices of entities that use their data, particularly those that are not covered by the HIPAA Privacy and Security Rules.

Three-Year Agenda: Send, Receive, Find, and Use Health Information to Improve Health Care Quality

We will develop an interoperability roadmap as articulated in HHS Principles and Strategy for Accelerating Health Information Exchange. Working with all stakeholders, we will fine-tune and use the health IT infrastructure enabled through implementation of the Health Information Technology for Economic and Clinical Health (HITECH) Act to support transformation of health care to a more patient-centered, less wasteful, and higher quality system. This near-term priority involves improving the interoperability of existing health information networks, and scaling existing approaches for fluidly exchanging health information across vendor platforms to support a broad array of transitions of care and public health. Ensuring that individuals and care providers send, receive, find, and use a basic set of essential health information[8] across the health care continuum will enhance care coordination and enable health system reform to improve care quality. This means focusing on query-based health information exchange, or the ability to appropriately search for and retrieve health information, in addition to point-to-point information sharing.

Through ONC's standards and certification processes, we will work to further standardize the vocabulary and structure of essential information. We will also address critical issues such as data provenance, data quality and reliability, and patient matching to improve the quality of interoperability, and therefore facilitate an increased quantity of information movement. Working with stakeholders, we will operationalize a common framework to enhance trust by addressing key privacy, security, and business policy and practice challenges to advance secure, authorized health information exchange across existing networks. Finally, we will work with federal and state entities to advance payment, policy, and programmatic levers that encourage use of this information in a manner that supports care delivery reform, improves quality, and lowers costs.

Six-Year Agenda: Use Information to Improve Health Care Quality and Lower Cost

Over the next six years, the care delivery system will realize enhanced interoperability. Health IT will continue to enable individuals to be active participants in managing their care as an important contributor of information to the health record (e.g., patient experience, self-rated health, and self-generated data). Individuals, care providers, and public health departments will send, receive, find and use an expanded set of health information across the care continuum to support team-based care. Care providers, such as those in schools, ambulances, and prisons will be able to appropriately exchange and use relevant health information.

Individuals look up their electronic immunization histories when needed.

Primary care providers share a basic set of patient information with specialists during referrals; specialists "close the information loop" by sending updated basic information back to the primary care provider.

Hospitals automatically send an electronic notification and care summary to primary care providers when their patients are discharged.

**These examples are meant as illustrations and are not meant to provide a comprehensive list.*

Figure 4. Example three-year agenda use cases.*

Remote monitoring will be enabled through better interoperability between medical devices, home-monitoring tools, and health information technology, including EHRs. Multi-payer claims databases, clinical data registries, and other data aggregators will incrementally become more integrated as part of an interoperable technology ecosystem.

Health care providers will also be able to aggregate and trend information within and across groups of patients based on information from multiple data sources to monitor health disparities and quality improvement opportunities (population health management). As value-based payment gains traction across Medicare, Medicaid, and commercial payers and purchasers, there will be new methods of measuring clinical quality that represent the most important aspects of care delivery and health outcomes. We will work with stakeholders to refine standards, policies, and services to automate the continuous quality improvement process and deliver targeted clinical decision support that fits into a clinician's workflow to close care gaps and improve the quality and efficiency of care.

Individuals regularly contribute information to their electronic health records for use by members of their care team.

Individuals integrate data from their health records into apps and tools that enable them to better set and meet their own health goals.

Primary care providers and authorized researchers are able to understand how well controlled diabetic patient population's glucose levels (i.e., A1C values) are and how often those patients have been hospitalized based on standardized information from multiple sources.

Clinical settings and public health are connected through bi-directional interfaces that enable seamless reporting to public health departments and seamless feedback and decision support from public health to clinical providers.

**These examples are meant as illustrations and are not meant to provide a comprehensive list.*

Figure 5. Example six-year agenda use cases.*

10-YEAR AGENDA: THE LEARNING HEALTH SYSTEM

By year 10, the nation's health IT infrastructure will support better health for all through a more connected health care system and active individual health management. Information sharing will be improved at all levels of public health, and research will better generate evidence that is delivered to the point of care. Advanced, more functional technical tools will enable innovation and broader uses of health information to further support health research and public health.

The evolution of standards, policies, and data infrastructure over the next 10 years will enable more standardized data collection, sharing, and aggregation for patient-centered outcomes research. Continuous learning and improvement will be feasible through analysis of aggregated data from a variety of sources. Health IT systems will enable both analysis of aggregated data and use of local data at the point of care through targeted clinical decision support (CDS). CDS will improve care by taking into account information such as an individual's genetic profile, local trends in disease prevalence, antibiotic resistance, occupational hazards, and other factors.

The process of clinical trial recruitment, data collection, and analysis will be accelerated and automated. Retrospective analyses will allow for rapid inquiry around many aspects of public health, health care quality, outcomes, and efficiency. Public health surveillance will be dramatically improved through better outbreak detection and disease incidence and prevalence monitoring. Interoperable health IT will also help contain outbreaks and manage public health threats and disasters.

> The nation's health IT infrastructure will facilitate health improvement through active individual health management, improved information sharing with public health, and the ability for research to generate evidence that is delivered to the point of care.

How Will We Get There?

It will take a strategic and focused effort by the federal government, in collaboration with state, tribal, and local governments and the private sector. We will aim to develop a shared agenda that focuses on five critical building blocks for a nationwide interoperable health information infrastructure:

1. Core technical standards and functions
2. Certification to support adoption and optimization of health IT products and services
3. Privacy and security protections for health information
4. Supportive business, clinical, cultural, and regulatory environments
5. Rules of engagement and governance

Individuals manage information from their own electronic devices and share that information seamlessly across multiple electronic platforms as appropriate (health care providers, social service providers, consumer-facing apps and tools, etc).

Primary care providers can select effective medications for patients with certain conditions based on their genetic profiles and results of comparative effectiveness research.

Individuals, care providers, public health and researchers contribute information and learn from information shared across the health IT ecosystem, with rapid advancement in methods for deriving meaning from data without sharing PHI.

** These examples are meant as illustrations and are not meant to provide a comprehensive list.*

Figure 6. Example 10-year agenda use cases.*

These building blocks are interdependent and progress must be incremental across all of them over the next decade to realize this vision. We will develop a more comprehensive set of use cases and goals for three, six and ten-year timeframes that will guide work in each of the building blocks, including alignment and coordination of prioritized federal, state, tribal, local, and private sector actions.

BUILDING BLOCK #1: CORE TECHNICAL STANDARDS AND FUNCTIONS

Through our Standards & Interoperability (S&I) Framework, ONC will continue to work with industry stakeholders and federal and state governments to advance core technical standards for terminology and vocabulary, content and format, transport, and security. These standards will enable, at a minimum, the following essential services for interoperability:

1. Methods to accurately match individuals, providers and their information across data sources
2. Directories of the technical and human readable end points for data sources so they and the respective data are discoverable
3. Methods for authorizing users to access data from the data sources
4. Methods for authenticating users when they want to access data from data sources
5. Methods for securing the data when it is stored or maintained in the data sources and in transit, i.e., when it moves between source and user
6. Methods for representing data at a granular level to enable reuse
7. Methods for handling information from varied information sources in both structured and unstructured formats
8. ONC will also work toward flexible and dynamic technical tools to support interoperability for primary and secondary use of health information, such as the architecture described in the JASON report prepared for the Agency for Healthcare Research and Quality, A Robust Health Data Infrastructure.

Building Block #2: Certification to Support Adoption and Optimization of Health IT Products and Services

ONC will leverage the ONC Health IT Certification Program to ensure that a broad spectrum of health IT conforms to the technical standards necessary for capturing and exchanging data to support care delivery. Certification will be used to test that health IT conforms to standards, and also to certify that the technology has the ability to interoperate with other data sources so that users can exchange and use information from other systems. To increase flexibility in our regulatory structure, ONC has proposed that content and transport functions of technology be tested for certification separately. ONC has also been responsive to a demand for expansion of the certification program's scope to include health IT used in a broader set of health care settings, such as long-term and post-acute care and behavioral health. Ensuring consistent adoption of standards and policies for health IT applications used across all settings of care will support interoperability and health information exchange.

BUILDING BLOCK #3: PRIVACY AND SECURITY PROTECTIONS FOR HEALTH INFORMATION

ONC will strive to ensure that privacy and security-related policies, practices, and technology keep pace with the expanded electronic exchange of information for health system reform. We will continue to assess evolving models of health information exchange to identify and, with stakeholder input, develop solutions to address weaknesses and gaps in privacy protections. We will encourage the development and use of policy and technology and workflow practices to advance patients' rights to access, amend, and make informed choices about the disclosure of their electronic health information. We recognize that there are certain state and federal laws under which some patients must give affirmative consent to the disclosure of their health information (often related to a "sensitive" health condition such as behavioral health or genetic information), a privacy protection that is more stringent than the HIPAA Privacy Rule. ONC will endeavor to ensure that these patients will not be left on the wrong side of the digital divide. We will work to improve standards, technology, and workflow that enable the electronic collection and management of consent as well as the electronic exchange of related information within existing legal requirements (including notice of redisclosure restrictions). We will also invest in methods and approaches that support distributed analytics and open evidence sharing without sharing PHI. Continued coordination across federal and state governments is needed to develop, implement, and evolve appropriate privacy and security policies for various types of health information exchange.

Expanding interoperability and exchange may also pose new security challenges. We will work with the National Institute of Standards and Technology (NIST) and other stakeholders to expand the options for ensuring, at an appropriate level of certainty, that those who access health information electronically are who they represent themselves to be. We will continue to assess and improve policies and standards that help ensure health information is only accessed by authorized people and is used in reasonable and transparent ways. We will also work with the private sector to address emerging cyber threats.

Given our support for electronic access by individuals to their own health information, we will also be mindful of the privacy and security risks created when information exits the realm of HIPAA covered entities. We will support developers creating health tools for consumers to encourage responsible privacy and security practices and greater transparency about how they use personal health information. In addition, we will collaborate with the Office for Civil Rights and other agencies to encourage greater consumer education about the benefits of health information exchange and the steps they can take to safeguard their own data.

As we expand health information exchange, it is important that all stakeholders (the government, health care providers and plans, vendors, developers, patients and their caregivers) recognize their responsibility in protecting health information. We intend to continue our outreach and technical assistance to help everyone reach this goal.

BUILDING BLOCK #4: SUPPORTIVE BUSINESS, CLINICAL, CULTURAL, AND REGULATORY ENVIRONMENT

While the Medicare and Medicaid EHR Incentive Programs have been a primary motivator for the adoption and use of certified EHR technology, these programs alone are insufficient to overcome barriers to our vision of information sharing and interoperability as outlined above. Current policies and financial incentives often prevent such exchange, even when it is technically feasible. To ensure that individuals and care providers send, receive, find, and use a basic set of essential health information across the care continuum over the next three years, we need to migrate policy and funding levers to create the business and clinical imperative for interoperability and electronic health information exchange.

In collaboration with employers, federal agencies, and private payers, ONC will help define the role of health IT in new payment models that will remove the current disincentives to information exchange. Incremental steps to accelerate health information exchange will initially stem from Affordable Care Act (ACA) delivery reform programs and Medicare payment regulations. HHS will consider ways in which the adoption and use of ONC-certified health IT products can be aligned with and encouraged by Medicare and

Medicaid payment policy, and other HHS programs funding health care delivery so that care delivery transformation and interoperability evolve in tandem.

With regard to individual access to health information and the engagement it enables, a significant barrier is a lack of knowledge among members of the public that access to health information is becoming increasingly available, and a cultural bias against taking advantage of it. Many patients are intimidated or embarrassed to ask for copies of their records or to ask health-related questions of their providers. To address these cultural barriers, we will encourage providers to proactively offer access to health information for their own patients, and using consistent marketing and messaging via the Blue Button Initiative, encourage diverse stakeholders including data holders and consumer advocacy organizations to educate individuals about their rights and the benefits of access to and use of health information.

We will also work with states, employers, consumers, providers, technology developers, payers, and others to support efforts driving appropriate health information exchange for improvements in care and to see that any regulatory and business barriers preventing data flow are reduced and/or removed.

BUILDING BLOCK #5: RULES OF ENGAGEMENT AND GOVERNANCE OF HEALTH INFORMATION EXCHANGE

The HITECH Act charged ONC with establishing a governance mechanism for the nationwide health information network.

We view the nationwide health information network as a continually expanding ecosystem of electronic exchange activities and network service providers across the nation that rely on a set of standards, policies, and services to meet electronic exchange needs including the privacy, security, and appropriate use of the information exchanged.

This market includes many forms of electronic exchange and network service providers, ranging from simple forms (such as direct electronic exchange of health information between two known providers) to more sophisticated forms (such as query and response techniques). Governance will facilitate trust and interoperability across all the diverse entities and networks that provide exchange services so that health information follows individuals regardless of where and when they access care.

LOOKING FORWARD

In 2014, ONC will build on our existing governance framework and principles to ensure individual access, privacy, transparency, responsible financial and business practices, and use of federal standards to support health information exchange. As needed, ONC will identify the "rules of the road" necessary for information to flow efficiently across networks and will transition to a governance approach for health information exchange that will likely involve both policy and collaboration across industry, government, and consumer representatives.

Experience has demonstrated that while trust can be established among specific, known groups of health information trading partners (providers, public health departments, payers, etc.) through local governance, data use agreements, and other contractual arrangements (constituting a trust community), scaling trust across communities requires assurance that each adheres to a minimum set of common security and business practices. Our governance approach must consider a common framework for privacy, security, technology, data, and business practices, provide assurance to trust communities that each abides by that framework (including a process for dispute resolution and reconciliation), and maintain minimum technical tools where needed to make scaling trust easy.

We will seek input and collaboration with federal agencies to inform governance implementation and ensure broad participation across existing operating health information networks, including those focused at the vendor, enterprise, regional, and state levels. We seek to promote competition among network service providers in a way that avoids providers or individuals being "locked in" to one mechanism to exchange health information, limiting their ability to share health information and coordinate care efficiently.

It will take time to build a fully interoperable infrastructure of coordinated care and communication across health care providers, patients, and public health entities that improves health care quality, lowers health care costs, and improves population health. HHS is fully committed to ensuring ubiquitous, standards-based interoperability of health information across all care settings through a multi-year approach that is consistent, incremental, yet comprehensive. No one person, organization, or government agency alone can realize this vision of an interconnected health system. But together, we can achieve the promise and potential of health information technology to improve the health of all.

End Notes

[1] Formally referred to as the Medicare and Medicaid EHR Incentive Programs.

[2] The term "care providers" is broadly inclusive of the care continuum, reflecting primary care providers, specialists, nurses, pharmacists, physical therapists and other allied care providers, hospitals, mental health and substance abuse services, long- term and post-acute care facilities, home and community-based services, other support service providers, care managers, and other authorized individuals and institutions.

[3] http://www.healthit.gov/facas/sites/faca/files/HITPC Data Analytics Update 2014-04-08.pdf.

[4] Office of the National Coordinator for Health Information Technology. 'U.S. Hospitals' Capability to Electronically Query Patient Health Information from Outside Their Organization and System,' Health IT Quick-Stat, no. 25. April 2014.

[5] http://healthit.gov/policy-researchers-implementers/state-hie-implementation-status.

[6] See http://bluebuttonconnector.healthit.gov/ to learn which data holders are offering electronic access to personal health data by consumers.

[7] See http://www.healthit.gov/policy-researchers-implementers/hie-bright-spots for examples of lessons and successes from recent health information exchange efforts.

[8] The basic set of essential health information builds from the common meaningful use (MU) data set incorporated into ONC's health IT certification program as part of the 2014 Edition EHR Certification Criteria and currently used to support three MU objectives included in the Medicare and Medicaid EHR Incentive Programs.

In: Connected Health Care
Editor: Elaine Ramirez

ISBN: 978-1-63484-947-0

Chapter 2

CONNECTING HEALTH AND CARE FOR THE NATION: A SHARED NATIONWIDE INTEROPERABILITY ROADMAP (FINAL VERSION 1.0)*

Office of the National Coordinator for Health Information Technology

LETTER FROM THE NATIONAL COORDINATOR

We live in an exciting moment for health information technology (health IT).

Today, rapid advancements in the field have led to new opportunities – everything from precision medicine to accountable care organizations. Best of all, improved health IT systems have led to newly engaged, empowered, and educated consumers.

But we know that not everyone in this country has access to the health IT they need to support high quality, personalized care. Our long term goal is simple: to build a strong foundation of health IT in our health care system, equipping every person with a long-term, digital picture of their health over their lifespan.

---

* This is an edited, reformatted and augmented version of document issued by the Office of the National Coordinator for Health Information Technology, December 2015.

We are closer than ever before. The exciting successes of today – and the bright future of tomorrow – are the result of more than a decade's worth of work by the private and public sector, bolstered by investment under the Health Information Technology for Economic and Clinical Health (HITECH) Act of 2009. Today, electronic health record adoption is the highest it has ever been, meaning that we are moving towards realizing the goal of every American having an electronic health record.

Exchange of information between health systems is flowing faster than ever before, and new technology innovations are bringing more usable digital health information to the bedside and beyond. We must build upon this success to create an open, person-centered health IT infrastructure – one that can support our neighbors not just as engaged patients, but as healthy citizens across their lifespan.

In *Connecting Health and Care for the Nation: A 10-Year Vision to Achieve an Interoperable Health IT Infrastructure* (ONC's 10-Year Interoperability Concept Paper)[1], we described our vision for how interoperability is necessary for a "learning health system" in which health information flows seamlessly and is available to the right people, at the right place, at the right time. Our vision: to better inform decision making to improve individual health, community health, and population health.

To complete this vision, I am pleased to issue the Final Version of the Shared Nationwide Interoperability Roadmap (the Roadmap). The Roadmap was informed by stakeholders nationwide to coordinate our collective efforts around health IT interoperability. And it describes the policy and technical actions needed to realize our vision of a seamless data system.

Public and private stakeholders will need to do more than just address our policies and technical approaches to achieve real, meaningful, seamless interoperability – we will need to change our culture. We will all need to commit to actions that will define how we work together on behalf of the American public to empower them to improve their health. We are committed to helping consumers easily and securely access their electronic health information when and where they need it most; to enabling individual health information to be shared with other providers and refrain from information blocking; and to implementing federally recognized, national interoperability standards and policies so that we are no longer competing between standards, but rather innovating on a set of core standards. We hope the private sector will join us in this pledge.

ONC is thankful to the individuals and organizations who shared their expertise and time to provide the feedback that was used to improve the

Roadmap. We read and listened to public comments from over 250 organizations on the draft Roadmap, including our federal partners, states, and ONC's Federal Advisory Committees (FACAs). Each of the milestones, calls to action, and commitments in this roadmap were informed and prioritized according to your feedback. Now it is time for all of us to bring these commitments to life by working together toward realizing a true learning health system by achieving the Roadmap's milestones – especially the foundational milestones that need to be accomplished by the end of 2017.

The Roadmap is a living document, and we intend to evolve it in partnership with the public and private sectors as technology and policy require. Thank you all in advance for your continued dedication and work on the advancement of nationwide interoperability as a means of creating an open, connected community, best able to serve the health needs of all Americans.

Karen B. DeSalvo, MD, MPH, MSc
National Coordinator for Health Information Technology

EXECUTIVE SUMMARY

The nation needs an interoperable health system that empowers individuals to use their electronic health information to the fullest extent; enables providers and communities to deliver smarter, safer, and more efficient care; and promotes innovation at all levels. While the Health Information Technology for Economic and Clinical Health (HITECH) Act stimulated significant health information technology (health IT) adoption and exchange of electronic health information with the goal of every American having access to their electronic health information, 2015's interoperability experience remains a work in progress. The vision is a learning health system where individuals are at the center of their care; where providers have a seamless ability to securely access and use health information from different sources; where an individual's health information is not limited to what is stored in electronic health records (EHRs), but includes information from many different sources (including technologies that individuals use) and portrays a longitudinal picture of their health, not just episodes of care; where diagnostic tests are only repeated when necessary, because the information is readily available; and where public health agencies and researchers can rapidly learn, develop, and deliver cutting edge treatments.

INTEROPERABILITY PROGRESS

2004

- National Coordinator for Health IT position created via Executive Order 13335
- Decade of Health IT: Delivering Consumer-centric and Information-rich Health Care: Framework for Strategic Action released

2005 to 2008

- Stark exception and anti-kickback safe harbor enable donations of health IT products and services
- American Health Information Community (AHIC) formed
- Health Information Technology Standards Panel (HITSP) formed
- Nationwide Health Information Network (NHIN) develops prototypes for exchange
- Certification Commission for Health Information Technology (CCHIT EHR certification program begins
- ONC-Coordinated Federal Health IT Strategic Plan 2008-2012
- Health Information Security and Privacy Collaboration formed across 42 states and territories
- State Alliance for e-Health

2009

- HITECH Act Passed
- 16% of hospitals and 21% of providers adopted basic EHRs
- Data Use and Reciprocal Support Agreement signed - enables exchange with federal agencies

2010

- State Health Information Exchange (HIE) Cooperative Agreement Program begins
- First ONC rule making for Health IT Certification program
- Blue Button Initiative, a tool that provides patients with access to their electronic health information, is launched
- Direct Project launched to enable a secure, standards-based way to electronically send health information to known, trusted recipients over the Internet

INTEROPERABILITY PROGRESS

2011

- Federal Health Information Technology Strategic Plan 2011-2015
- Meaningful Use Stage 1 begins
- 27% of hospitals and 34% of providers adopted EHRs
- Blue Button Initiative Pledges from the Private Sector begin 2012

2012

- The Consolidated Clinical Document Architecture (CDA), a unified standard for summary care records is created
- Healtheway is launched

2013

- CommonWell, an industry-led Network Service Provider, is launched
- 51% of hospitals can electronically query other organizations for health information
- The Department of Health and Human Services (HHS) HIE Acceleration Strategy Released

2014

- Carequality, a public-private collaborative, is formed
- The Argonaut project is launched to develop a first-generation Fast Healthcare Interoperability Resources (FHIR) based application programming interface and core data specification
- A 10-Year Vision to Achieve an Interoperable Health IT Infrastructure released
- 80% of hospitals can electronically query other organizations for health information
- Meaningful Use Stage 2 attestations began

2015

- The Draft Shared Nationwide Interoperability Roadmap 1.0 released for public comment
- Additional State HIE Cooperative Agreement funds awarded for breakthrough innovations
- Federal Health IT Strategic Plan 2015-2020 released
- The 2015 Interoperability Standards Advisory released

If we steadily and aggressively advance our progress we can make it a reality. We must focus our collective efforts around making standardized, electronic health information securely available to those who need it and in ways that maximize the ease with which it can be useful and used.

The Office of the National Coordinator for Health IT (ONC) is committed to advancing this vision expeditiously, systematically and in a sustainable fashion. We first laid out this vision in Connecting Health and Care for the Nation: A 10-Year Vision to Achieve an Interoperable Health IT Infrastructure and followed with a draft Shared Nationwide Interoperability Roadmap and Interoperability Standards Advisory. Working collaboratively with federal partners, states, consumers, and the private sector, we developed this shared, comprehensive interoperability agenda and action plan described in detail in the Shared Nationwide Interoperability Roadmap (the Roadmap). It is meant to build upon and shore up the existing foundation of health IT, move quickly to short-term success, and also lay out a longer term set of drivers and policy and technical components that will achieve the outcomes necessary to achieve the vision. ONC will continue to work with our partners as we coordinate the Roadmap's implementation, which is also a critical part of achieving the Federal Health IT Strategic Plan's vision of high-quality care, lower costs, healthy population, and engaged people.

The Roadmap identifies near-term (i.e., by the end of 2017) actions and roles that health IT stakeholders should perform to make immediate progress and impacts with respect to interoperability. It also emphasizes that we should use and build on the technology and investments made to date, while continuing to seek out ways to support innovation and move beyond EHRs as the sole data source for electronic health information to a wide range of health information technologies used by individuals, providers, and researchers. The Roadmap's three high-level goals for health IT interoperability each reflect the progress we need to make in order to achieve a learning health system by 2024. Consequently, the short-term goal is focused on sending, receiving, finding, and using priority data domains, so that we can have an immediate impact on the care and health of individuals.

The goals are:

- **2015-2017:** Send, receive, find and use priority data domains to improve health care quality and outcomes.
- **2018-2020:** Expand data sources and users in the interoperable health IT ecosystem to improve health and lower costs.

- **2021-2024:** Achieve nationwide interoperability to enable a learning health system, with the person at the center of a system that can continuously improve care, public health, and science through real-time data access.

The Roadmap focuses deeply on the first priority goal and its accompanying milestones, critical action items, and commitments. To address current challenges, the Roadmap identifies four critical pathways that health IT stakeholders should focus on now in order to create a foundation for long-term success:

- Improve technical standards and implementation guidance for priority data domains and associated elements. In the near-term, the Roadmap focuses on using commonly available standards, while pushing for greater implementation consistency and innovation associated with new standards and technology approaches, such as the use of APIs.
- Rapidly shift and align federal, state, and commercial payment policies from fee-for-service to value-based models to stimulate the demand for interoperability.
- Clarify and align federal and state privacy and security requirements that enable interoperability.
- Coordinate among stakeholders to promote and align consistent policies and business practices that support interoperability and address those that impede interoperability.

The Roadmap is organized into three sections starting first with "***Drivers***," which are the mechanisms that can propel development of a supportive payment and regulatory environment that relies on and deepens interoperability. The next section addresses "***Policy and Technical Components***," which are essential items stakeholders will need to implement in similar or compatible ways in order to enable interoperability, such as shared standards and expectations around privacy and security. The last section addresses "***Outcomes***," which serve as the metrics by which stakeholders will measure our collective progress on implementing the Roadmap. Each section includes specific milestones, calls to action, and commitments that will support the development of a nationwide, interoperable health IT infrastructure.

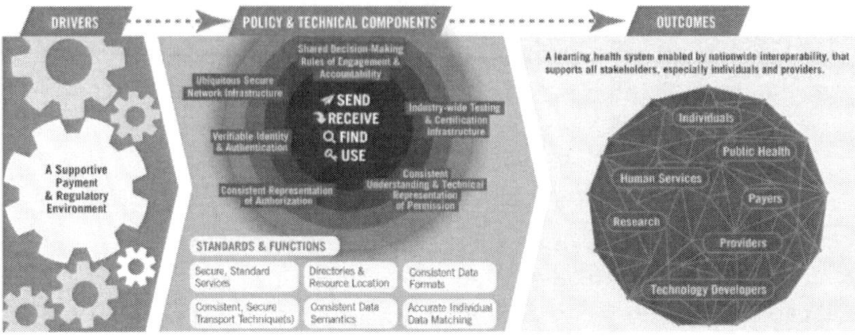

The Roadmap is intended to be a living document. As we move forward to create a learning health system, the Roadmap will be updated and new versions will be created when milestones are met and new challenges emerge. Future Roadmap versions will continue to be informed by and incorporate stakeholder feedback. ONC's website will list calls to actions and commitments mapped out by stakeholder group so that all stakeholders can identify and do their part.

ROADMAP INTRODUCTION

Interoperability: the ability of a system to exchange electronic health information with and use electronic health information from other systems without special effort on the part of the user.[2]

Purpose of the Roadmap

In 2014, the Office of the National Coordinator for Health Information Technology (ONC) published *Connecting Health and Care for the Nation: A 10-Year Vision to Achieve an Interoperable Health IT Infrastructure*,[3] which described a vision for the improvement of health information technology (health IT) interoperability in three-, six- and 10-year time increments. *A Shared Nationwide Interoperability Roadmap version 1.0* (Roadmap), the second paper in the *Connecting Health and Care for the Nation* series, uses the same three-, six- and 10-year increments to clearly guide stakeholder focus in the near- and long-term and to catalyze collaboration among public and private stakeholders to achieve the vision. The Roadmap lays out a clear path for stakeholders who are going to build and use the health IT infrastructure.

In April 2015, Congress declared it, "…a national objective to achieve widespread exchange of health information through interoperable certified EHR technology nationwide by December 31, 2018."[4] The milestones, calls to action and commitments to be achieved by 2017 support this objective. In addition, the Roadmap's implementation is a critical part of the *Federal Health IT Strategic Plan 2015-2020* (Strategic Plan),[5] specifically Goal 4 (see Figure 1). The Roadmap directly aligns with the Plan's mission of improving the health and well-being of individuals and communities through the use of technology and health information that is accessible when and where it matters most. The Strategic Plan focuses on federal actions and strategies to broaden and modernize the Nation's health IT infrastructure to support each of the four goals. While the Plan focuses on federal efforts, the Roadmap details the policy, technology and behavioral changes that public and private stakeholders must make to achieve nationwide interoperability.

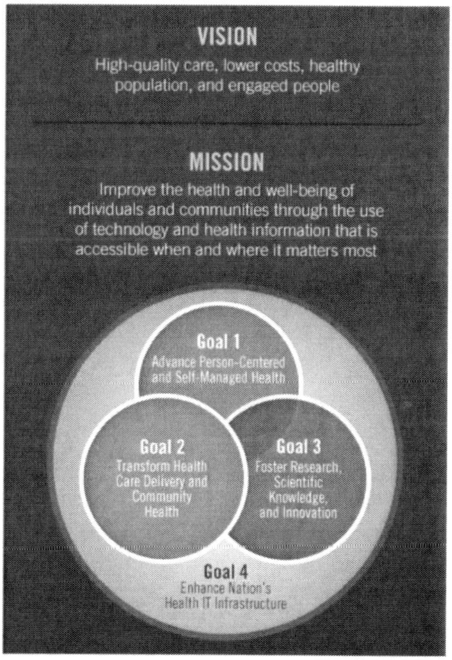

Figure 1. Federal Health IT Strategic Plan: Vision, Mission and Goals.

Current State

While the adoption of electronic health record (EHR) systems has seen a dramatic increase in the last five years, the nation has yet to see widespread interoperability between those systems. Health information exchange, however, is occurring in many pockets of the country. Today, approximately 41 percent of hospitals nationwide routinely have electronic access to necessary clinical information from outside providers or sources when treating an individual. Last year, approximately 78 percent of hospitals electronically sent a summary of care document and 56 percent received a summary of care document. However, less than half of hospitals are integrating the data they receive into an individual's record.[6] Additionally, as of 2013, only 14 percent of ambulatory providers shared electronic health information with providers outside of their organization.[7] While progress has been made over the last few years, there is still significant work for stakeholders to undertake to build nationwide interoperability.

Interoperability Vision for the Future

For purposes of this Roadmap, interoperability is defined as the ability of a system to exchange electronic health information with and use electronic health information from other systems without special effort on the part of the user.[8] This means that all individuals, their families and health care providers should be able to send, receive, find and use electronic health information in a manner that is appropriate, secure, timely and reliable to support the health and wellness of individuals through informed, shared decision-making. With the right information available at the right time, individuals and caregivers can be active partners and participants in their health and care. An interoperable health IT ecosystem should support critical public health functions, including real-time case reporting, disease surveillance and disaster response. Additionally, interoperability can support data aggregation for research, which can lead to improved clinical guidelines and practices. Over time, interoperability will also need to support the combining of administrative[9] and clinical data to enhance transparency and enable value-based payment. The work and collaborative efforts of all stakeholders over the next 10 years will yield interoperability achievements in a variety of areas that, in turn, will advance the industry toward a learning health system.

A learning health system is an ecosystem where all stakeholders can securely, effectively and efficiently contribute, share and analyze data. A learning health system is characterized by continuous learning cycles, which encourage the creation of new knowledge that can be consumed by a wide variety of electronic health information systems. This knowledge can support effective decision-making and lead to improved health outcomes. A learning health system includes a broad array of stakeholders that extend beyond the clinical care delivery system. This could include routine and emergency transactions from public health services among governmental agencies such as state and local health departments, emergency responders and public safety; hospitals; health care professionals; diagnostic laboratories; researchers; non-governmental human services; advocacy and community based organizations. A learning health system also incorporates advanced health models that increasingly leverage technology. For example, telecommunications technology can be used to remotely deliver health and health care services and improve access to care across clinical and non-clinical community settings; and medical device data, which represents the largest source of objective biometric and clinical data can improve real-time diagnostics and treatment of the critically ill. Interoperability provides the underpinning infrastructure that is fundamental to enabling a learning health system.

Scope

The Roadmap is intended for health IT stakeholders who will build the infrastructure necessary for interoperability and for those who will use that infrastructure. This iteration of the Roadmap focuses primarily on actions that will enable a majority of individuals and providers across the care continuum to send, receive, find and use priority data domains at the nationwide level by the end of 2017 (see figure 7 *in H. Consistent Data Semantics*). Although the near-term target focuses on individuals and care providers, it is important to ensure the priority data domains are standardized to support community-based services, human services, public health and the research community. Also in-scope for the Roadmap is the ability to use data to support better stratification across populations of aggregated electronic health information to identify and address health disparities, support research and evidence-based precision medicine.

The interaction between clinical and administrative electronic health information is a critical concern, but not every facet of interoperability can be handled in this iteration of the Roadmap. While administrative data is out of scope for the Roadmap at this time, it is clear that a learning health system must eventually encompass both administrative and clinical health information. Use cases, standards, technologies and tools that leverage both administrative and clinical electronic health information will be an important topic to address in future iterations of the Roadmap and the health IT ecosystem should experiment in this area.

There are also many aspects of health IT beyond interoperability that are important and will be critical to supporting a learning health system, including technology adoption, data quality, usability and workflow. In an attempt to draw a boundary around "interoperability," many aspects of these topics are out of scope for this Roadmap. For example, the capability of an EHR to accept and parse a standard clinical document is "in scope" for the Roadmap because it is critical to interoperability. However, the user's experience in interacting with that clinical document or its data within the EHR – while critically important – falls outside the boundary of interoperability in the Roadmap's context. Similarly, while clinical decision support (CDS) algorithms and alerts that a user might experience within an EHR are out of scope, the application programming interfaces (APIs) and data transport techniques that may be called by a CDS service are *in scope*. Though this boundary is not hard and fixed and may evolve over future iterations of the Roadmap, it is important that the initial scope be manageable. Where appropriate, stakeholders should address some of these out-of-scope items within their own priorities and capabilities and should broadly share results and progress in public forums.

A Learning Health System:

"…will improve the health of individuals and populations. The learning health system will accomplish this by generating information and knowledge from data captured and updated over time – as an ongoing and natural by-product of contributions by individuals, care delivery systems, public health programs, and clinical research – and sharing and disseminating what is learned in timely and actionable forms that directly enable individuals, clinicians, and public health entities to separately and collaboratively make informed health decisions…
The proximal goal of the learning health system is to efficiently and equitably serve the learning needs of all participants, as well as the overall public good."

Taken from the *Learning Health Community's Preamble*

Figure 2. A Learning Health System.

Stakeholders Involved in Interoperability

A broad range of people and organizations traditionally involved in clinical care delivery and many outside the clinical care delivery system who impact the health of individuals are all pivotal to achieving interoperability among a broad range of needs. The Roadmap denotes the stakeholder groups who are best positioned to take on a critical action or that directly benefit from actions to be taken. In most cases, individuals, groups and organizations will fit more than one stakeholder perspective. Furthermore, professional organizations that represent the interests of a particular stakeholder may identify with one or more stakeholder perspective. The following list is an effort to identify those who in some way can affect (or are affected by) interoperability. The term "stakeholder" will be used throughout the Roadmap to reference this broader category. The term "health IT stakeholder" will be used to reference those who directly affect interoperability.

- **People who receive care or support the care of others:** Individuals, consumers, patients, caregivers, family members serving in a non-professional role and professional organizations that represent these stakeholders' best interests.
- **People and organizations that deliver care and services:** Professional care providers who deliver care across the continuum, not limited to but including hospitals, ambulatory providers, pharmacies, laboratories, behavioral health including mental health and substance use disorder treatment services, home and community based services, nursing homes and professional organizations that represent these stakeholders' best interests.
- **Organizations that pay for care:** Private payers, employers and public payers that pay for programs like Medicare, Medicaid and TRICARE.
- **People and organizations (governmental) that support the public good:** Federal, state, tribal and local governments.
- **People and organizations that generate new knowledge, whether research or quality improvement:** Researchers, population health analytics and quality improvement knowledge curators and quality measure stewards.
- **People and organizations that provide health IT capabilities:** Technology developers for EHR and other health IT, including but not limited to health information exchange (HIE) technology, laboratory

information systems, personal health records, pharmacy systems, mobile technology, medical device manufacturers, telecommunications and technologies to enable telehealth, and other technology that provides health IT capabilities and services, which includes health information exchange organizations (HIOs) and clearinghouses.

- **People and organizations that govern, certify and/or have oversight:** Governing bodies and accreditation/certification bodies operating at local, regional, or national levels that provide a governance structure, contractual arrangements, rules of engagement, best practices, processes and/or assess compliance.
- **People and organizations that develop and maintain standards:** Standards development organizations (SDOs) and their communities of participants, such as technology developers, health systems, providers, government, associations, etc.

Guiding Principles for Nationwide Interoperability

ONC originally articulated a set of guiding principles and building blocks in *Connecting Health and Care for the Nation: A 10-Year Vision to Achieve an Interoperable Health IT Infrastructure.*[10] Based on feedback from a wide range of stakeholders, ONC has updated these principles as listed below. The principles guide the development of critical actions and strategies to advance interoperability in the future. They are intended to focus our collective efforts to make practical and valuable progress, while encouraging innovation. These principles align with the Plan principles (listed first below), and expand upon them with principles that are specific to interoperability rather than the broader scope of health IT advancement.

1. **Focus on value.** Strive to make sure our interoperability efforts yield the greatest value to individuals and care providers. Improved health, health care and lower costs should be measurable over time and at a minimum, offset resource investment.
2. **Be person-centered.** Members of the public are rapidly adopting technology, particularly mobile technology, to manage numerous aspects of their lives, including health and wellness. However, many of these innovative apps and online tools do not yet integrate electronic health information from the care delivery system.

Electronic health information from the care delivery system should be easily accessible to individuals and empower them to become more active partners and participants in their health and care.

3. **Protect privacy and security in all aspects of interoperability and respect individual preferences.** It is essential to maintain public trust that health information is safe and secure. To better establish and maintain that trust, stakeholders will strive to ensure that appropriate, strong and effective safeguards for electronic health information are in place as interoperability increases across the industry. Stakeholders will also support greater transparency for individuals regarding the business practices of entities that use their data, particularly those that are not covered by the HIPAA Privacy and Security Rules, while considering the preferences of individuals.
4. **Build a culture of electronic access and use.** Standards and methods for achieving interoperability must be accessible nationwide and capable of handling significant and growing volumes of electronic health information, to ensure no one is left on the wrong side of the digital divide.
5. **Encourage innovation and competition**. Demand for interoperability from health IT users is a powerful driver to advance our vision. The market should encourage innovation to meet evolving demands for interoperability.
6. **Build upon the existing health IT infrastructure.** Significant investments have been made in health IT across the care delivery system and in other relevant sectors that need to exchange electronic health information with individuals and care providers. To the extent possible, stakeholders should build from existing health IT infrastructure, increasing interoperability and functionality as needed.
7. **One size does not fit all.** Although interoperability requires technical and policy conformance among networks, technical systems and their components, it does not require that each stakeholder implement exactly the same technology. Stakeholders will strive for baseline interoperability across health IT infrastructure, while encouraging innovation that improves usability.
8. **Simplify.** Where possible, simpler solutions should be implemented first, with allowance for more complex functionality in the future.
9. **Maintain modularity.** A large, nationwide set of complex, scalable systems are more resilient to change when they are divided into independent components that can be connected together. Because

medicine and technology will change over time, stakeholders must preserve systems' abilities to evolve and take advantage of the best of technology and health care delivery. Modularity creates flexibility that allows innovation and adoption of new, more efficient approaches over time without overhauling entire systems.

10. **Consider the current environment and support multiple levels of advancement.** Not every individual or clinical practice will incorporate health IT into their work in the next 3-10 years and not every practice will adopt health IT at the same level of sophistication. Stakeholders must therefore account for a range of capabilities among information sources and information users, including EHR and non-EHR users, as stakeholders advance interoperability. Individuals and caregivers have an ongoing need to send, receive, find and use their own health information both within and outside the care delivery system.

How the Roadmap is Organized

The Roadmap is organized into three main sections as shown above: drivers, policy and technical components and outcomes that should be met and measured as we achieve interoperability for many different needs (Figure 3). The drivers are the incentives that promote interoperability. Policy and technical components are the items that must be in place to enable interoperability. Consistent and compatible policy and technical components must be implemented by stakeholders to achieve interoperability nationwide. Additionally, the policy and technical components are all essential and each one must be achieved to enable interoperability. Lastly, as we achieve interoperability for different needs, we need to do so with a measurement framework that focuses on measuring improved outcomes for all stakeholders involved, especially individuals and providers. Note that the section list below is not meant to be a prioritization. Rather, the letters are used as a key for readers to quickly identify milestones, calls to action and commitments associated with each section.

Drivers

A. A supportive payment and regulatory environment

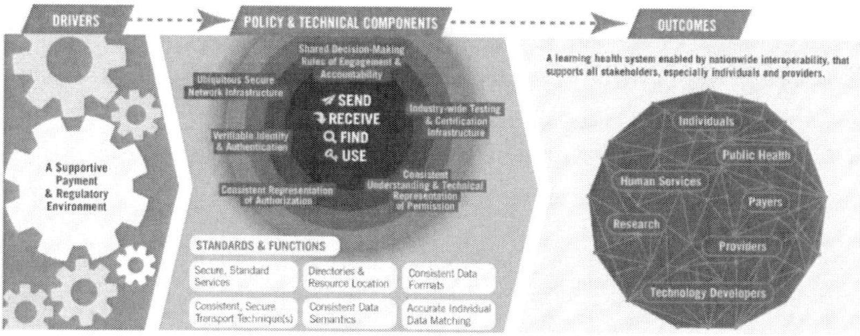

Figure 3. How the Roadmap is Organized.

Policy and Technical Components

B. Shared decision-making, rules of engagement and accountability
C. Ubiquitous, secure network infrastructure
D. Verifiable identity and authentication of all participants
E. Consistent representation of authorization to access electronic health information
F. Consistent understanding and technical representation of permission to collect, share and use identifiable health information
G. Industry-wide testing and certification infrastructure
H. Consistent data semantics
I. Consistent data formats
J. Standard, secure services
K. Consistent, secure transport technique(s)
L. Accurate individual data matching
M. Health care directories and resource location

Outcomes

N. Individuals have access to longitudinal electronic health information, can contribute to that information, and can direct it to any electronic location
O. Provider workflows and practices include consistent sharing and use of patient information from all available and relevant sources

Achieving nationwide interoperability that enables a learning health system will take a strategic and focused effort by the private sector in collaboration with federal, state, tribal and local governments. Throughout the Roadmap, each section includes high-level historical context, a current state and a desired future state. Each section also includes milestones for each timeframe, indicating what should be achieved by when. Each section has a table associated with it at the end of the document that lists milestones by timeframe (reiterated from the main body), priority calls to action and priority commitments across three-, six- and 10-year timeframes (See Complete Set of Calls to Action and Commitments by section). The calls to action and commitments support achievement of the milestone for each timeframe, and ultimately, each milestone supports the overarching goal of each timeframe.

- **Milestones** are indicators that help us see if we are on track to reach interoperability. For example, the milestones listed in each section in the 2015-2017 timeframe align to the first timeframe goal of send, receive, find and use priority data elements to improve health and health care.
- **Calls to action** are opportunities where stakeholders can take the lead in and commit to as participants. Calls-to-action are prioritized actions that support achievement of the milestones.
- **Commitments** are prioritized actions that stakeholders have publicly committed to fulfilling. Commitments support achievement of the milestones.

Figure 4. Milestones, Calls to Action and Commitments.

Process for Updating the Roadmap

The Roadmap is intended to be a living document that is guided in its evolution by all health and health care stakeholders. ONC will continue to coordinate efforts and engage with stakeholders to publish future iterations. However, the owners of the Roadmap are the stakeholders represented herein. We have considered and included feedback from the many stakeholders who commented on the draft version of the Roadmap that was published for public comment in January 2015. The final version 1.0 of the Roadmap was revised using that feedback to more clearly describe the actions needed to achieve our collective interoperability goals. ONC anticipates updating the Roadmap every two years with broad input from the public, stakeholders and its federal advisory committees (FACAs), the HIT Policy Committee (HITPC) and HIT Standards Committee (HITSC).

Additional Resources

While the Roadmap contains important details on each business and functional requirement for nationwide interoperability to enable a learning health system, there is a significant amount of background that sits behind this document. For more background detail on health IT, as well as the drivers, policy and technical components and outcomes, please see the Supplemental Materials document that accompanies the Roadmap.

Shared Nationwide Interoperability Roadmap

Drivers

A. A Supportive Payment and Regulatory Environment

Rules that govern how health and care are paid for must create a context in which interoperability is not just a way to improve care, but is a good business decision.

Background and Current State

Shifting payment models to those that pay for quality versus quantity is pivotal to creating the business imperative for interoperability. While the Medicare and Medicaid EHR Incentive Programs have been a primary motivator for the adoption and use of certified EHR technology among specific groups of clinicians,[11] these programs alone are insufficient to overcome barriers to the Roadmap's vision for information sharing and interoperability. The current business environment does not adequately reward, and often inhibits exchange of electronic health information, even when it is technically feasible. History has shown that without the right financial incentives in place, systems and technology components are built and not used.

While important progress is being made today, the health care landscape continues to be dominated by fragmentation in care delivery and payment models that are largely based on the volume of services delivered, rather than the delivery of efficient, high-quality care and better patient outcomes. When providers are rewarded for value, interoperability can be a significant tool to help them meet such requirements, but broad demand for interoperability has lagged and been insufficient to drive connectivity across health care providers. Providers that are increasingly accountable for patient outcomes and total cost of care, regardless of where else that individual has received care, will increasingly demand access to an individual's complete clinical record, laboratory results, broader health-related information (human service and other community-based information) and total cost of care required to effectively manage the person's health.

As models that reward quality over quantity continue to expand, providers are more likely to see a business case for making the time and cost investments to incorporate use of interoperable health information into how they deliver care. This, in turn, will increase the demand for interoperable technology.

The Medicare Access and CHIP Reauthorization Act (MACRA), signed by the President in April 2015, will take important steps toward streamlining and expanding the use of value-based payment and quality reporting programs. Set to phase in over a number of years, MACRA will consolidate current physician reporting programs, including the Medicare and Medicaid EHR Incentive Program, into a unified Merit-Based Incentive Payment System (MIPS).

MACRA also creates a new bonus framework for providers that participate in certain Alternative Payment Models (APMs) outside of traditional fee-for-service Medicare (beginning in 2021, APMs established by commercial payers will also contribute to the threshold providers must meet.) Under the law, eligible APMs will need to include a downside risk feature and a quality measurement framework and will also require participating providers to utilize certified health IT as part of the model. Through its health IT provision, MACRA will reinforce the link between value-based payment and the use of certified technology to coordinate care. As these programs integrate providers across care settings, these requirements are likely to reach a provider base that includes critical providers ineligible for the Medicare and Medicaid EHR Incentive Program, such as many post-acute care providers. In addition, the link to value-based payment promises to incentivize providers to invest in resolving interoperability challenges in their communities.

Movement to alternative payment models will naturally stimulate demand for interoperability. In addition, a supportive payment and regulatory environment must lower real and perceived costs of interoperability. Today, many providers may choose not to share data for a variety of reasons beyond technology capabilities, including concerns around the increased liability risk of exchanging data, competing technology priorities or a lack of ready trading partners. In other cases, providers may believe interoperability will jeopardize competitive advantages they gain from exclusive access to patients' health information. Likewise, technology developers may contribute to high interoperability costs by making it challenging for providers to extract and share data, for instance, in order to prevent providers from easily switching to a competitor's product.

Moving Forward and Critical Actions

To create a payment and regulatory environment that drives providers to value interoperability, all stakeholders who pay for health and health care must explore opportunities to accelerate interoperability because it is a key supporter of broader efforts to move toward a value-based health care system. While the transition to new ways of paying for care will ultimately stimulate demand for interoperability in the long run, there are many actions that stakeholders can take in the short and medium term to accelerate interoperable exchange of electronic health information.

As the nation's largest purchaser of health care, the federal government can exercise considerable leverage across the care delivery system by linking payment with the use of electronic health information exchange and certified health IT. As described in the 2013 statement, "Principles and Strategy for

Accelerating Health Information Exchange," HHS is committed to a natural lifecycle of policies to drive interoperability beginning with incentives, followed by payment adjustments and then conditions of participation in Medicare and Medicaid programs.[12] For instance, HHS will explore opportunities to promote interoperability through increasing participation in value-based payment. In January 2015, HHS Secretary Burwell announced a set of delivery system reform goals to tie payment to how well providers care for their patients, instead of how much care they provide. A key goal of this initiative is to have 85 percent of all Medicare fee-for-service payments tied to quality or value by 2016, and 90 percent by 2018. Another key target is to have 30 percent of Medicare payments tied to alternative payment models by the end of 2018 and 50 percent of payments by the end of 2016.[13]

In addition to the federal government, states, private payers and purchasers of insurance also play a significant role in shifting the payment and regulatory environment through incentives, payment reform initiatives, and contracting processes. States have considerable opportunities to support interoperability, especially through the administration of state Medicaid programs and their ability to direct how Medicaid funds are spent. CMS has identified a number of ways that states can use Medicaid funds to develop care coordination capacity among their Medicaid providers, and several states have already begun to use Medicaid Managed Care contracts to advance interoperability.[14] Health plans can also promote interoperability among provider networks. In parallel with public sector efforts over the past several years, commercial health plans have developed and deployed a wide range of value-based payment programs within their provider networks that offer new opportunities to focus attention on and generate demand for interoperability. Finally, private purchasers of health care, including large employers, can use their market power to advance interoperability by working with and encouraging health plans to adopt these initiatives within their own geographic regions.

The following includes milestones for a Supportive Payment and Regulatory Environment. Please see the Complete Set of Calls to Action and Commitments by Roadmap Section at the end of this document for the critical actions that need to take place to advance nationwide interoperability.

Milestones for a Supportive Payment and Regulatory Environment

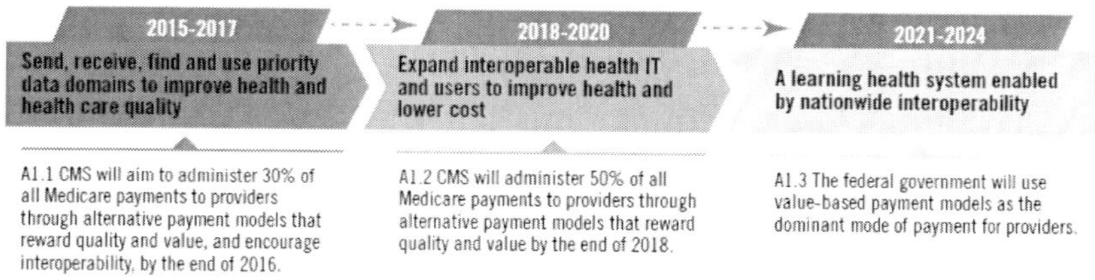

Policy and Technical Components

B. Shared Decision-Making, Rules of Engagement and Accountability

Nationwide interoperability across the diverse health IT ecosystem will require stakeholders to agree to and follow a common set of standards, services, policies and practices that facilitate the appropriate exchange and use of health information nationwide and do not limit competition. Once established, maintaining interoperability will also require ongoing coordination and collaborative decision-making about future change.

Background and Current State

Establishing a common set of standards, services, policies and practices is best accomplished through an inclusive and transparent process that sets priorities, makes decisions, establishes authorities and rules of engagement and ensures accountability. This activity is often referred to as "governance." Governance processes also help establish trust between disparate data trading partners and build confidence in the practices of the other people or organizations with whom electronic health information is shared. The term "governance" has often been misinterpreted in the context of electronic health information interoperability, thus we use it sparingly in this and other sections of the Roadmap.

Individuals are not stationary – they change jobs and thus health insurance networks, relocate to different states and seek care from providers beyond defined technical networks.[15] Therefore, electronic health information must flow across technology developer, geographical and organizational boundaries in a manner that supports individuals' health and care. It must also support individuals' access to their information and their ability to share that information with other individuals and entities. Consequently, the processes by which trust is established must be scalable and extensible over time.

Electronic Health Information Sharing Arrangements

A number of electronic health information sharing arrangements, such as health information exchanges (HIE), networks and trust communities currently exist. Electronic health information sharing arrangements are used to enable interoperability between otherwise unaffiliated organizations or parties. These arrangements typically include single or multiple agreements between parties on rules of engagement for information sharing (how information will be shared, purposes for which it can be used, baseline security practices, etc.) and how those rules can be changed. They also describe accountability mechanisms that make parties comfortable sharing information (such as surveillance mechanisms, audit logs and recourse when the rules are not followed) or providing access to their technical systems and agreement on the standards that will be used. These electronic health information sharing arrangements often have overlapping regional, state or national footprints, and all have contributed to a significant increase in the exchange of electronic health information. For example, CommonWell Health Alliance is, "creating and executing a vendor-neutral platform that breaks down the technological and process barriers that currently inhibit effective health data exchange. And…[is] committed to defining and promoting a national infrastructure with common standards and policies."[16] The Sequoia Project (formerly Healtheway) manages the Carequality initiative which is developing common rules of the road, technical specifications, and a participant directory to enable cross-network exchange.[17] The Sequoia Project also manages eHealth Exchange, which is working to, "improve patient care, streamline disability benefit claims, and improve public health reporting through secure, trusted, and interoperable health information exchange."[18] DirectTrust is working to, "develop, promote and, as necessary, help enforce the rules and best practices necessary to maintain security and trust within the Direct community, and to foster widespread public confidence in the Directed exchange of health information."[19]

Despite the potential and intention of existing electronic health information sharing arrangements, they differ from each other in fundamental ways that make it difficult for them to work together. They often have differing immediate goals and differing methods or standards to achieve those goals. Some networks that support health care, implement information sharing arrangements through formal contracts or legal data sharing and use agreements,[20] while some rely on self-attestation or independent accreditation.[21] Some operate technical testing programs while others do not. And most, but not all, operate some level of technical infrastructure. The result can be a complex web of electronic health information sharing arrangements that creates some degree of interoperability within specific geographic regions, organizational and technology developer boundaries, but fail to produce seamless nationwide interoperability to support a learning health system.[22] These existing arrangements, that are often one-to-one contracts or data use agreements, are unlikely to scale nationwide and may not be extensible to new, novel data uses that support health.

Efforts to Bridge Electronic Health Information Sharing Arrangements

Moving forward successfully with shared decision-making, rules of engagement and accountability requires an understanding of what has been tried in the past. ONC has made several attempts to overcome variation across existing electronic health information sharing arrangements to enable nationwide interoperability, but with limited success. Efforts to promote the adoption of common standards, policies and practices nationwide to advance shared decision making and rules of engagement were attempted through both the American Health Information Community (AHIC)[23] and the National eHealth Collaborative (NeHC). However, neither effort had the ability to compel participation in nor to enforce compliance with their decisions, rules or accountability mechanisms. Without this ability, electronic health information sharing arrangements cannot advance interoperability.

The HITECH Act[24] directed ONC to establish a governance mechanism for the nationwide health information network (NwHIN).[25] Industry response to ONC's request for information (RFI)[26] on the topic indicated a general desire for ONC to refrain from formal governance activity at that time and to allow nascent and emerging governance efforts in industry to take shape. In lieu of any regulatory action on NwHIN governance, ONC pursued a variety of initiatives to build consensus among a broad range of stakeholders through collaborative efforts. This included issuing the *Governance Framework for Trusted Health Information Exchange (HIE)*,[27] which established guiding principles on HIE governance and collaborating with states[28] and existing HIE governance entities.[29] While these collaborative efforts advanced some aspects of interoperability, they have not yielded nationwide interoperability. In some cases the projects were experimental and in other cases, such as the governance framework, there was nothing to compel or incent its use.

Moving Forward and Milestones

ONC continues to believe that the electronic health information sharing arrangements described above are valuable tools to promote interoperability among unaffiliated organizations. However, there are evident gaps, overlaps and conflicting approaches among and between the various organizations that prevent the sharing of electronic health information. Reaching the near- and long-term nationwide interoperability goals will require existing arrangements to be able to share information across their respective boundaries, even between competitors, and should focus on the Roadmap's near term goal of sending, receiving, finding and using priority data domains.[30]

In a country as large and heterogeneous as the U.S., it is not realistic to suggest that all electronic health information needs will be met with a single electronic health information sharing arrangement. Therefore, a variety of electronic health information sharing arrangements will continue to exist as they serve important market and clinical functions that meet the unique needs of many different communities. While each electronic health information sharing arrangement may continue to use its own policies, service agreements and technical standards to support participant priorities and needs, a common set of policies and technical standards must be adopted across the ecosystem to bridge disparate arrangements and support nationwide interoperability. This will provide electronic health information users the flexibility to use services with deep, local, electronic health information sharing functions that meet many of their day-to-day needs, while having the confidence that they can still engage in key universal transactions with any authorized users in any network. Along with the flexibility described above, nationwide interoperability will require more than has been done to date to support shared decision making, rules of engagement and accountability to enable trust.

In addition to the shared decision-making process, an enduring set of principles to align practices across all electronic health information sharing arrangements and a method of knowing who abides by those principles must be created. Public and private sector stakeholders should use policy guidance issued by ONC as a starting point for these efforts. These stakeholders will also need to work together to establish a common shared decision-making process where operational level issues related to standards, services, policies and business practices that inhibit the achievement of interoperability across existing and new electronic health information sharing arrangements can be resolved. This process should address mechanisms for accountability, including identifying and addressing those who are out of compliance with policies and practices. The process should be inclusive and balance the participation of all stakeholders.

The following includes milestones for Shared Decision-Making, Rules of Engagement and Accountability to Enable Interoperability. Please see the

Complete Set of Calls to Action and Commitments by Roadmap Section at the end of this document for the critical actions that need to take place to advance nationwide interoperability.

Milestones for Shared Decision-Making, Rules of Engagement and Accountability

C. Ubiquitous, Secure Network Infrastructure

Enabling an interoperable, learning health system requires a stable, trusted, secure, widely available network capability that supports technology developer-neutral protocols and a wide variety of core services.

Background and Current State

The security of network infrastructure is pivotal to ensuring the success of nationwide interoperability to enable a learning health system. It serves as the basis for trust by ensuring that electronic health information can be shared in a secure and private manner and not altered in an unauthorized or unintended way, while still making the information available when needed by those authorized to access it. The security of health IT systems and their underlying security infrastructure will continuously evolve as necessary to maintain its secure state as critical infrastructure.[31]

As health IT systems have become increasingly connected to each other, cyber threats have concurrently increased at a significant rate.[32] In an interoperable, interconnected health IT ecosystem, an intrusion in one system could allow intrusions in multiple other systems. Additionally, there is high variability in the capabilities and resources that health care organizations have at their disposal to prevent cyberattacks. Large organizations often have the resources and expertise to have a dedicated information security team to address cybersecurity, while small and mid-sized organizations may not have those same resources. There is also a significant need for behavioral and cultural change across the health IT ecosystem regarding cybersecurity. Many in health care do not realize the significant risk to their health IT systems and do not understand the importance and urgency of implementing security best practices to prevent cyber-attacks. Despite being identified as critical infrastructure for the nation, the health care industry could do more to prepare for cyber-attacks.[33]

Data encryption (scrambling or encoding data so that it cannot be read without the appropriate credential) is a fundamental cybersecurity control. This helps ensure that data can be exchanged and stored in a trusted manner. Encryption can be applied when data is sent (in transit), particularly over networks like the Internet that are not otherwise secure, and when it is stored (at rest). For encryption to work, the system or program using the information must be able to decrypt it. For example, a key may be used to reverse the process and change the encrypted information back into the original information. The security of the encryption key must be maintained for the encrypted data to remain secure. In particular, the procedures by which encryption keys are generated, distributed, stored, rotated, and revoked must be secure and access should be tightly controlled.[34]

Encryption is also a safe harbor provision under the HIPAA Breach Notification Rule.[35] This means that if a HIPAA Covered Entity (CE) or Business Associate (BA) (e.g., a cloud-based EHR and data services provider who may have custody of the electronic protected health information (ePHI)) chooses to encrypt ePHI consistent with guidance in the HIPAA Breach Notification Rule[36] and discovers a breach of that encrypted information, neither a CE nor a BA is required to provide the breach notifications specified in the Rule. See Supplemental Materials document for more information on cybersecurity and encryption.

Moving Forward and Milestones

Cybersecurity depends on security controls and best practices, including but not limited to:

- Create and maintain a security risk management program.
- Maintain contracts, such as Data Use Agreements, Memoranda of Understanding/Memoranda of Agreement (MOU/MOA), Interconnection Security Agreements, and Business Associate Agreements (BAA). These documents are typically contracts between two parties that are in addition to each party's own internal compliance documents such as HIPAA privacy and security policies

and procedures. These documents will need to scale beyond bi-lateral contracts to support nationwide interoperability.

- Share threat information across organizations and develop mature incident response capabilities.
- Perform operational & behavioral monitoring of user credentials, administrator credentials, and use of system credentials, particularly those credentials that have system-level access to APIs or databases that contain ePHI or individually identifiable health information (IIHI).
- Ensure that health IT is developed and deployed securely, following Department of Homeland Security (DHS)[37] and National Institute of Standards and Technology (NIST)[38] guidance for building security into health IT products, not just putting products behind a secure exterior.
- Assess the security of applications and infrastructure via penetration testing, potentially conducted by third party experts, to identify vulnerabilities before they are exploited.
- Encrypt the contents of all network messages in transit even if it is not legally required.
- Secure all data stored in any database connected to the network, whether through a companion system, interface engine or gateway, by encrypting data at rest and securing the encryption keys.
- Participate in bug bounty programs.

Breaches can occur outside the control of data stewards. Fraud and medical identity theft occurred in health care long before information technology systems were introduced. However, health IT systems are vulnerable to breaches, such as zero-day vulnerabilities, which when present in underlying operating systems may lead to compromised infrastructure. While not all breaches of ePHI can be prevented, the list above along with other best practices recommended by NIST, the Office for Civil Rights (OCR) and others can reduce both the amount and scope of data breaches, and allow individuals and organizations to recover faster when breaches do occur.

The following includes milestones for Ubiquitous, Secure Network Infrastructure. Please see the Complete Set of Calls to Action and Commitments by Roadmap Section at the end of this document for the critical actions that need to take place to advance nationwide interoperability.

Milestones for Ubiquitous, Secure Network Infrastructure

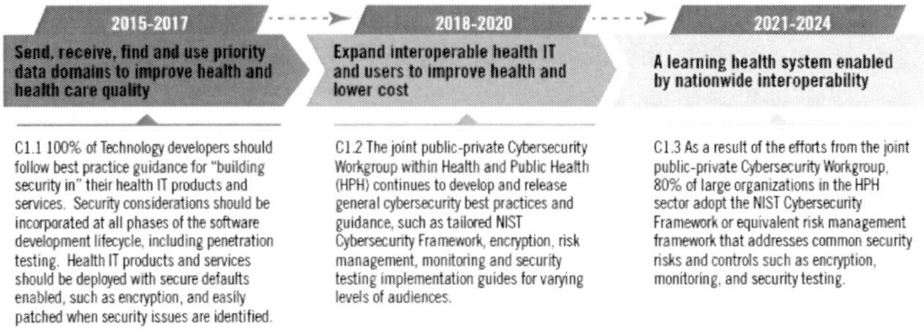

D. Verifiable Identity and Authentication of All Participants

Legal requirements and cultural norms dictate that users of systems—whether people or machines—be known so that access to data and services is appropriate. This is a requirement for all participants in nationwide interoperability that supports a learning health system regardless of their role (e.g., individual, patient, provider and administrator).

Background and Current State

Nationwide interoperability requires that all participants, regardless of role (e.g., individual, provider, researcher), be identified and authenticated to access a system so there is a high level of trust that participants cannot fraudulently pose as someone else. Identity proofing is the process of verifying that a user is who they say they are and binding a technical credential to that identity. Authentication occurs when an individual or system uses a credential, such as a username and password, to access a system (Figure 5).

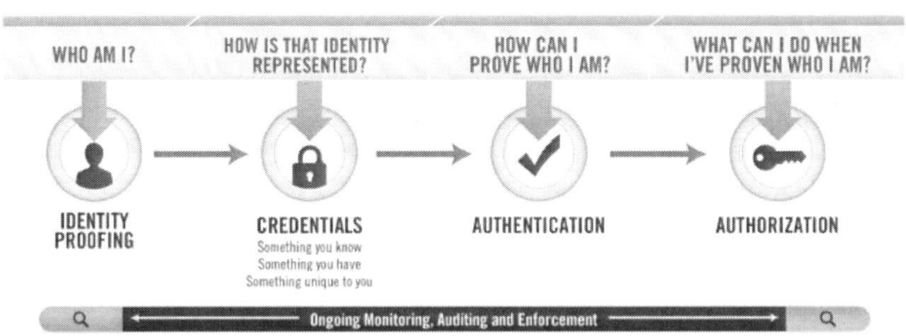

Figure 5. Identity Management & Authorization Concepts.

Appropriate identity proofing and authentication policies, processes and technologies can help individuals trust that their electronic health information and other data are secure and private. Many electronic health information holders, technology developers and network service providers have been unwilling to exchange electronic health information or allow access to their systems without assurance that trading partners have acceptable processes for identity proofing and compatible authentication methods. The HIPAA Security Rule includes an authentication standard[39] that requires CEs to implement procedures to verify that a person or entity seeking access to ePHI is the one claimed. NIST Special Publication 800-63-2 defines several levels of assurance (LoA), ranging from one to four, that outline requirements for establishing trustworthy identity proofing and authentication. Higher risk functions and services, such as access to electronic health information, require a higher LoA.

The lack of consistently applied methods and criteria for both identity proofing and authentication has significantly hampered the exchange of electronic health information across organizations. For example, Direct was intended to work much like email and lower the barrier to exchange for providers and hospitals by eliminating the need for complex legal agreements between individual organizations. However, many network service providers, such as HISPs, have different identity proofing and authentication policies or requirements and may not acknowledge the identity proofing and authentication undertaken by other HISPs or network service providers. This effectively limits the organizations with which a provider can share electronic health information.

National Strategy for Trusted Identities in Cyberspace (NSTIC)

In 2010, NSTIC was launched as a public-private collaborative to help, "individuals and organizations utilize secure, efficient, easy-to-use and interoperable identity credentials to access online services in a manner that promotes confidence, privacy, choice and innovation."[40] Over the last few years NSTIC has developed pilots to test various electronic means for ensuring identity and authenticating users. The intent of these efforts is to develop an identity ecosystem that can mitigate cybersecurity issues, which are not unique to health care, while maintaining the privacy of individuals. NSTIC's overarching goal is the elimination of passwords because, "usernames and passwords are broken; most people have 25 different passwords, or use the same one over and over,"[41] creating system vulnerabilities and increasing identity theft.[42] A recent Executive order encouraged alignment with NSTIC by federal agencies.[43]

HIT Policy Committee (HITPC) Recommendations

Over the last three years, the HITPC Privacy and Security Tiger Team has put significant effort into providing recommendations that address both provider and individual identity proofing and authentication issues. Their recommendations strongly encourage the use of NIST LoA 3 for authenticating providers to remotely access ePHI.[44, 45] LoA 3 mandates high confidence in the asserted identity's accuracy, multi-factor authentication and identity proofing procedures that include the verification of identifying materials and information. For individual or patient authentication, the HITPC recommended that health IT augment password-based systems with knowledge-based attributes or other similar controls to strengthen authentication systems. Knowledge-based attributes are similar to security questions that users have to answer to recover a password.

Moving Forward and Milestones

To advance interoperability that enables a learning health system, providers and hospitals need to exchange electronic health information with any other provider or hospital that is appropriately identity proofed and authenticated, especially when directed by an individual to do so. Additionally, providers' systems need to recognize each other as authentic, and not nefarious, when the two systems connect for automated processes, like exchanging data through APIs. Similarly, authentication controls used by individuals and their personal representatives must be secure, easy-to- use, and intuitive so that authentication and identity proofing do not become roadblocks to individuals accessing their own electronic health information. Health care organizations' security risk analysis must take into account the varied levels of access that individuals, providers and health IT administrators have. For example, an individual accessing their electronic health information in a portal represents a lower risk than providers or health IT administrators that have much broader system access.

The use of mobile phones, email and other factors for authentication has become commonplace in many sectors such as banking and e-commerce. With the emergence of Internet accessible medical devices, monitors and the evolving Internet of Things,[46] mobile devices may be used in the future to identity proof and authenticate a patient and their associated devices at the point of care. This in turn could serve to promote a person-centric environment that would minimize the need for intermediaries to facilitate trust.

Additionally, gaps should be addressed so that victims of medical identity fraud have clear avenues of redress. Communication, outreach and educational activities should be used to support medical identity fraud victims. For example, the FTC has published consumer information regarding identity theft[47] and the Veterans Affairs (VA) campaign, "VA's More Than a Number", educates veterans and their beneficiaries on ways to protect themselves from identity theft.[48] There are some simple steps the nation can take to advance interoperability that enables the learning health system: establish standard identity proofing practices at the point of care; increase public awareness; leverage existing mobile technologies and smart phones to provide efficient, effective paths for patient or provider identity authentication; and establish policies and procedures that account for situations in which devices are unavailable (e.g., stolen, malfunction, etc.).

The following includes milestones for Verifiable Identity and Authentication of All Participants. Please see the Complete Set of Calls to Action and Commitments by Roadmap Section at the end of this document for the critical actions that need to take place to advance nationwide interoperability.

Milestones, Calls to Action and Commitments for Verifiable Identity and Authentication of All Participants

E. Consistent Representation of Authorization to Access Electronic Health Information

When coupled with identity verification, this allows consistent decisions to be made by systems about access to information.

Background and Current State

This section covers the general concept of authorization which is defined as the scope of information a person or system is allowed to access. This general concept of authorization is distinct from an “Authorization,” which refers to a signed permission document from an individual to a CE allowing it to use or disclose PHI for certain purposes.[49]

After an information requestor has been successfully authenticated, the information discloser must confirm what information the user is authorized to access or use. The determination that a requestor is authorized to access or use electronic health information is a legal matter that can be defined by the proposed use of the information (e.g., treatment, payment, and health care operations purposes as defined in the HIPAA Privacy Rule are often referred to as TPO),[50] the role of the proposed data user, an individual’s documented choice, or some combination of all three. Each information discloser is responsible for ensuring that a requestor’s access to electronic health information is appropriate and authorized. Information requestors and information disclosers can include a person or a health IT system.

Today, potential trading partners negotiate complex contracts before allowing access to electronic health information because, among other security and policy issues, they do not feel confident in each other’s authorizations to access or receive ePHI. A lack of widely-adopted technical standards to communicate authorization across the health IT ecosystem also impedes interoperability in healthcare (although the financial services sector seems to have mastered this.). This may be due to the diverse legal and regulatory environment discussed in the *Consistent Understanding and Technical Representation of Permission to Collect, Share and Use Identifiable Health Information* requirement. Currently, technical standards, such as Security Assertion Markup Language (SAML) and OAuth 2.0 can be used to electronically exchange computable assertions of authorization for access to electronic health information, when the trading partners agree as to what authority is required. New standards, such as OAuth 2.0, that are applicable across a broader set of sectors are evolving and being tested to consistently communicate authorization today.

Moving Forward and Milestones

Nationwide interoperability that enables a learning health system requires a reliable way to confirm authorization through consistently implemented technical standards that indicate when an asserted authorization to receive or access an individual’s electronic health information is accurate and can be trusted. This allows both an information requestor and information holder to have a common understanding of what is authorized. It is unlikely that cross-provisioning of users will happen between all organizations’ systems that need to provide access to or share electronic health information. That is, human users are not expected or required to have identities defined in all systems or security domains outside of the domain initiating a request. This highlights the importance of technical tools to assert authorization and compute it properly. Consistently implemented technical standards will allow authorization decisions to be automated. This in turn supports privacy compliance and the development of standardized APIs, improving efficiency and lowering cost across the entire ecosystem. Once APIs meet standard security requirements, developers must ensure that they are open and accessible, which will help rapidly scale interoperability.

Technical standards for authorization must account for access by different authenticated users, including providers, public health professionals, individuals and others. The authority for each user to access or use electronic health information will vary because of changing and complex roles, laws, regulations and an individuals' choices. Approaches to authorization must at a minimum 1) account for the legal, regulatory and individual choice environment, 2) unambiguously identify types of information users and the scope of their roles, and 3) clearly identify interdependencies between authorization and authentication, as there is a critical connection between these two distinct, but related process steps.

The following includes milestones for Consistent Representation of Authorization to Access Data or Services. Please see the Complete Set of Calls to Action and Commitments by Roadmap Section at the end of this document for the critical actions that need to take place to advance nationwide interoperability.

Milestones for Consistent Representation of Authorization to Access Data or Services

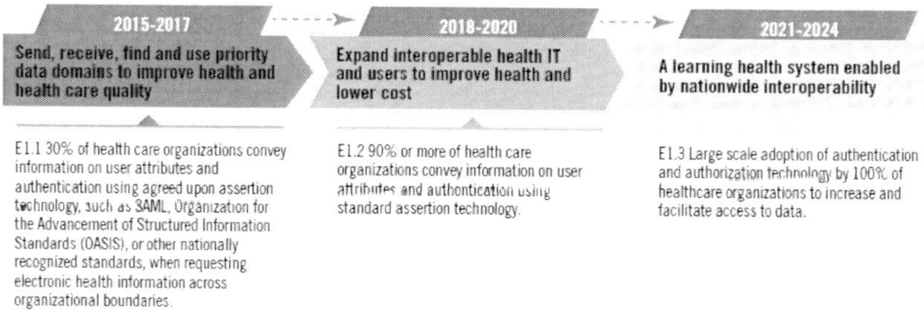

F. Consistent Understanding and Technical Representation of Permission to Collect, Share and Use Identifiable Electronic Health Information

Though requirements differ across states, nationwide interoperability requires a consistent way to represent legal permission to collect, share and use individually identifiable electronic health information, including with whom and for what purposes.

Background and Current State

The success of health IT and interoperability is dependent on individuals' trust that their electronic health information will be kept private and secure and that their rights related to this information will be respected. This is commonly thought of as permission to collect, share and use (including exchange) an individual's health information. These "permissions" impact interoperability in three ways: statutes and regulations, organizational policy and technology. Comments on the draft Roadmap demonstrated that there is a great deal of confusion about when PHI legally can be exchanged without a written permission; whether written permission is ever required for health information to be exchanged electronically versus in other media; when an individual's written permission is required for exchange; and about diverse and specialized state privacy laws. Each of these problems is discussed in detail in the Supplemental Materials document. In the end, removing confusion of all types will advance nationwide interoperability.

With advances in computing, technology could be harnessed to improve privacy compliance, and therefore trust. Certain aspects of the privacy landscape, however, cause confusion and impede our ability to harness technology to help.[51] Removing confusion is an important step to enabling technology in support of privacy compliance and trust.

Statutes and Regulations

Statutes and regulations set legal privacy protections for health information. At the federal level, the HIPAA Rules and their implementing regulations set a national baseline of health information privacy and security protections applicable to health plans, most health care providers and health care clearinghouses, as well as their BAs. The HIPAA Privacy Rule also provides rights for individuals to obtain access to their PHI[52] and rules governing when PHI may be used or disclosed without the individual's express written permission.[53] HIPAA is based on the Fair Information Practice

Principles (FIPPs).[54] See the Supplemental Materials document for more information on the FIPPs.

The HIPAA Privacy Rule generally permits the use or disclosure of PHI for limited specific purposes (such as treatment, payment, and health care operations – often referred to as TPO) without an individual's permission. HIPAA Rules support electronic exchange of health information in an automatic way, with rules that run "in the background." This ensures our nationwide care delivery system continues to function. How PHI is shared "in the background" without written permission is made transparent to individuals through Notices of Privacy Practices.[55]

Privacy laws also exist that have heightened privacy protections and require documented, written permission from individuals to share, use or disclose, certain types of health information. Some examples of federal regulations that contain these special protections are the Federal Confidentiality of Alcohol and Drug Abuse Patient Records regulations that apply to substance use treatment information[56] generated by federally funded programs that identify themselves as providing those services,[57] and federal laws protecting certain types of health information coming from covered U.S. Department of Veterans Affairs facilities and programs.[58]

Many states have their own laws and regulations to protect the privacy of health information, and these often have stricter privacy protections and requirements on use and disclosure than the HIPAA Privacy Rule. These statues and regulations vary from state-to-state, often narrowly targeting a particular population, health condition, information collection effort or specific type(s) of health care organizations. These diverse state laws are philosophically aligned towards preventing health-status discrimination. The laws' content, however, varies widely. The variation causes confusion among exchange partners, and makes it difficult and expensive to harness technology to ensure privacy compliance. This, in turn, impedes interoperability.

Organizational Policy

Organizational policies are internal rules, usually designed to comply with federal and state laws and managerial preferences, for how the organization will use and disclose electronic health information. The HIPAA Privacy Rule requires health care organizations to implement administrative policies and procedures. Organizational policies may and often do require certain procedures and restrictions on information use and disclosure that are more stringent than is required by law. Despite HIPAA's support of exchange of electronic health information for TPO, CEs may, and often do, voluntarily choose to obtain an individual's written consent prior to exchange as permitted by HIPAA. However, these more stringent organizational policies regarding the sharing of electronic health information should not impede interoperability.

Technology

Technological advances are creating opportunities to automate privacy compliance by tracking when ePHI can be used, accessed or disclosed. If the rules being processed are a clear "Yes" (okay to disclose) or a clear "No" (not okay to disclose), technology can be programmed to support privacy compliance.[59] ONC refers to this as computable privacy,[60] the technical representation and communication of permission to share and use identifiable health information, including when law and applicable organizational policies enable information to be shared without need to first seek an individual's permission. Once implemented effectively, using technology for privacy compliance saves time and resources, and can build trust and confidence in the system overall.

Moving Forward and Milestones

The U.S. legal, regulatory and policy landscape for sharing electronic health information is complex. While the laws are designed to protect health information, individual rights and to enable appropriate information sharing to support health and health care, other laws may not support both sets of goals. Despite efforts to address potential technology standards and solutions for documenting what permissions exist and communicating those permissions when needed to exchange, it has become clear that the complexity of the legal environment will continue to hinder the development and adoption of nationwide technology to support privacy compliance.[61]

To most effectively remove confusion about permission to share, use and disclose (exchange) electronic health information, we will have to harmonize these diverse, but philosophically aligned, laws. Through the course of harmonization, however, individual privacy rights as specified in state and federal laws must not be substantively weakened or eroded. (See the Supplemental Materials for a deeper discussion of Basic and Granular Choice).[62] With less confusion and ambiguity, we will be able to harness computing power to improve privacy compliance and fortify trust. With clarity and computing power, individuals who want to document detailed, granular privacy choices will be able to do so.[63]

The milestones, calls to action and commitments reflect ONC's and other stakeholders' best thinking about what should be done to improve understanding, harmonize rules and bring the capabilities of computer technology to areas such as enabling individuals to document their permissions electronically such that those permissions can be honored appropriately, nationwide, in circumstances where they are required.

The following includes milestones for Consistent Understanding and Technical Representation of Permission to Collect, Share and Use Identifiable Electronic Health Information. Please see the Complete Set of Calls to Action and Commitments by Roadmap Section at the end of this document for the critical actions that need to take place to advance nationwide interoperability.

Milestones for Consistent Understanding and Technical Representation of Permission to Collect, Share and Use Identifiable Electronic Health Information

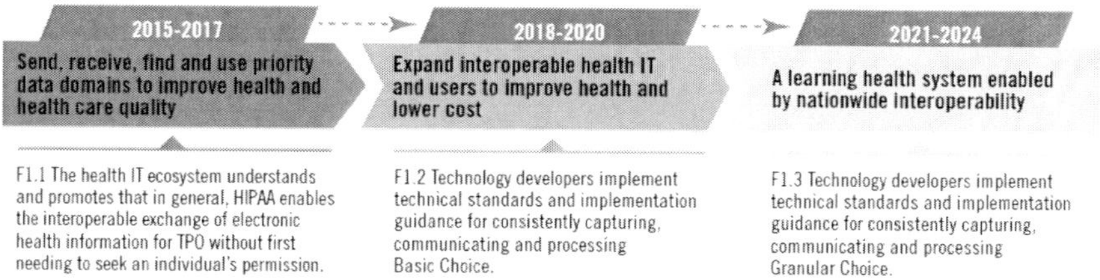

G. An Industry-wide Testing and Certification Infrastructure

A variety of health IT testing tools and resources must be broadly available to stakeholders to support technology from development through deployment. Testing and certification programs must provide health IT users with reasonable assurance that health IT is interoperable.

Background and Current State

Testing and certification can serve a variety of purposes when it comes to enabling nationwide interoperability. Testing and certification can increase market confidence in the safety of health IT products; accelerate the development and commercialization of technology; and enable standards developers, technology developers and users to evaluate technical implementations for inconsistencies and unexpected behaviors among other issues. Health IT testing can be administered in several different ways to evaluate technical functionality, standards implementation, and system performance. Testing can include, but is not limited to: self-testing, conformance testing, connect-a-thons and testing overseen by independent third-parties. While testing can be performed on its own, certification includes both testing and an additional review by an independent third-party who certifies that a product meets specific requirements. Certification is designed to provide confidence to stakeholders who may not have the technical expertise to evaluate whether a product meets specific requirements. Both testing and certification are necessary to support the optimization of health IT products and services for nationwide interoperability to enable a learning health system. In 2005, ONC funded the Certification Commission for Health Information Technology (CCHIT) to create the first voluntary health IT certification program. In 2009, the HITECH Act[64] provided the National Coordinator with the authority to establish a program or programs for the voluntary certification of health IT. To date, the certification criteria adopted by the Secretary have been correlated with and support Meaningful Use objectives and measures specified under the Medicare and Medicaid EHR Incentive Programs. During the last several years, additional health IT testing and certification programs have been developed, often specific to a use case or set of standards. Some examples include Surescripts' certification for ePrescribing, IHE Connect-a-thons for IHE profiles, EHNAC and DirectTrust programs for Direct services, HIMSS ConCert certification for SOAP-based query and Direct specifications, and many others. Additionally, the defense and intelligence industries use the Common Evaluation Methodology (CEM) for historical Common Criteria evaluations.

Moving Forward and Milestones

A diverse and complementary set of testing and certification programs will need to be in place to achieve nationwide interoperability. As legal, technical, regulatory and market forces reinforce the need for interoperability beyond organizational and network boundaries, testing and certification programs will help rapidly scale and promote trading partners' ability to consistently share and compute electronic health information using common technical standards. These testing and certification programs will need to be invested in and administered by a variety of different stakeholders both inside and outside of government. They will also need to be well-coordinated so as not to create conflicting or duplicative requirements for industry stakeholders.

Testing

To reach nationwide interoperability, the health IT ecosystem will need to invest in more efficient ways to test health IT that is implemented and used among a diverse set of stakeholders, such as network technologies and resources, payer systems, quality measurement, provider and consumer-facing applications, population health resources and others. Testing tools and resources should consistently focus on testing during health IT development, implementation, post-implementation and use. This will require broad industry commitment to the development, maintenance and use of testing tools. Negative testing and exception handling cases should be incorporated into unit testing to ensure systems are resilient across a broad range of real world interoperability scenarios. Finally, health IT users should be able to easily and regularly assess the core interoperability functions and performance of their products or services. For example, users should be able to evaluate a system's ability to send, receive, find and use data elements within the priority data domains for the use cases they need to carry out.

Certification

Certification programs, including but not limited to ONC's, should be established and based on health IT users' need for assurance about the performance of certain health IT products and services. To advance interoperability, certification programs should include a sufficient level of testing rigor around core interoperability functions, such that stakeholders derive a tangible benefit from the certification. The addition of transparent surveillance processes can protect purchasers of certified products and services as well as keep them up-to-date regarding poor performing or non-compliant products.

The following includes milestones for an Industry-wide Testing and Certification Infrastructure. Please see the Complete Set of Calls to Action and Commitments by Roadmap Section at the end of this document for the critical actions that need to take place to advance nationwide interoperability.

Milestones for an Industry-wide Testing and Certification Infrastructure

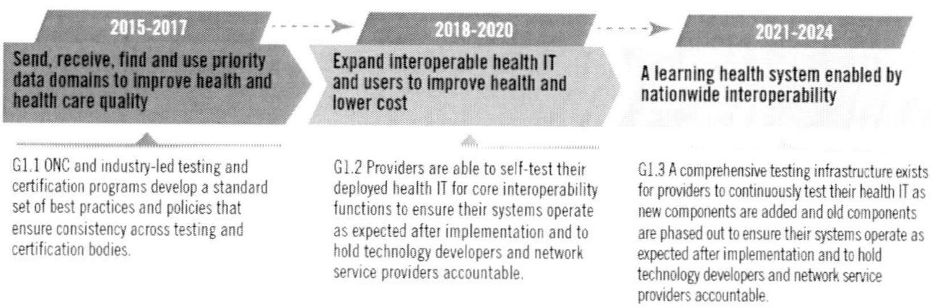

Standards and Functions Overview

To fully support the interoperability needs of a learning health system, core technical standards must be widely deployed and iteratively improved. The health IT ecosystem must reduce the amount of duplicative standards that hamper interoperability and consistently implement common standards that enable specific interoperability functions. Doing so will simplify standards compliance, minimize data mapping, improve cost efficiencies for technology developers and support a vibrant and entrepreneurial health IT market. Health IT standards often accommodate the complexity inherent in medicine and the business of health care. In general, standards are developed in response to a specific clinical or business need which is often referred to as a use case. Standards are also specified at different levels and combined in different ways to properly address user needs and expected data requirements. Typically five types of standards, with the accompanying implementation specifications, are necessary and used together to achieve interoperability for a given purpose (see Figure 6):

1. **Vocabulary/terminology standards** are sometimes unique to health care and use case-specific (e.g., codes to represent medications cannot be also used for laboratory tests).
2. **Content/format standards** are also often unique to health care and may be use case-specific for things like data capture or computation within a specific clinical workflow or domain (e.g., the content/ format standard used for a referral to a specialist would not be used to bill for a procedure).
3. **Transport standards** are typically not unique to health care because they are used to connect two or more parties together without a focus on the data that is transported from one party to another.
4. **Security standards** are not unique to health care and often applied in different ways to meet given data protection requirements. However, in health care there are legal minimums for functional security outcomes that are stated in the HIPAA Security Rule. In any event, a security standard supports achieving those security outcomes prescribed by the Security Rule. These standards are discussed in the privacy and security protection sections C through F.

5. **Standards for services** typically represent technical infrastructure used to connect different systems together to perform actions that support user needs. These are discussed further in Section J. Secure, Standard Services and include, but are not limited to APIs that enable systems to talk to each other.

Standards Development Organizations and Implementation Guidance

Standards Development Organizations (SDOs) act as convening bodies for the stakeholder communities that collaboratively develop, curate and maintain standards and information models including those mentioned above. These organizations include, but are not limited to: Health Level 7 (HL7), the National Council for Prescription Drug Plans (NCPDP), Integrating the Health care Enterprise (IHE), Clinical Data Interchange Standards Consortium (CDISC), Regenstrief Institute, International Health Terminology Standards Development Organisation (IHTSDO) and International Organization for Standardization (ISO). In addition to publishing standards, these organizations also create profiles or implementation guides that provide additional implementation instruction and examples for developers. For instance, the HL7 2.5.1 messaging standard is a content standard for which several different implementation guides have been created to address specific purposes ranging from laboratory result receipt to immunization submission.

CATEGORIES OF STANDARDS	FUNCTIONS OF STANDARDS	EXAMPLES OF REAL WORLD USE OF THE STANDARDS
VOCABULARY & CODE SETS (SEMANTICS)	The information is universally understood	RxNorm Code for Ibuprofen is 5640
FORMAT, CONTENT & STRUCTURE (SYNTAX)	Information is in the appropriate format	C-CDA packages up data in the appropriate format
TRANSPORT	The information moves from point A to point B	SMTP and S/MIME to send the C-CDA from one setting to another
SECURITY	The information is securely accessed and moved	X.509: to ensure it is securely transmitted to the intended recipient
SERVICES	Provides additional functionality so that information exchange can occur	DNS+LDAP: to find the recipient's X.509 certificate to encrypt a message

Figure 6. Standards Categories.

In some cases, the implementation guides provide sufficient clarity and specific implementation instructions as well as reducing the potential for implementation variability to a minimum. In other cases, further work is necessary among SDOs to further refine implementation guidance and develop best practices to improve implementation consistency among technology developers. The use of examples to reduce ambiguity and tools to facilitate conformance testing are also critical adjuncts to successful implementation within and across sites and systems.

H. Consistent Data Semantics

As electronic health information is shared and used among different stakeholders, its meaning must be consistently maintained in order to maximize its usage and value in a learning health system.

Background and Current State

The clinical vocabularies and coding systems used to represent clinical information in a health IT system are often referred to as data "semantics." Semantic interoperability is the "ability to automatically interpret the information exchanged meaningfully and accurately in order to produce useful results as defined by the end users of both systems." If sending and receiving systems are not developed and configured to adhere to a common and consistent set of vocabularies, code sets and value sets, the users of those systems will have difficulty with interoperability. For example, a health professional would readily understand that "Tylenol" and "acetaminophen" are generally used interchangeably. However, two computer systems exchanging those phrases may treat the terms entirely differently if the systems are not bound to a standardized vocabulary or terminology that equates them as synonyms. If two systems do not agree the terms are synonyms, then data passing through them will not be equally interpreted without additional effort.

Several vocabulary and terminology standards are already adopted by the Secretary in regulation and are required in the 2015 Edition.[65] These include but are not limited to:

- Systematized Nomenclature of Medicine-Clinical Terms (SNOMED CT) for problems or conditions;
- RxNorm for medications and medication allergies;
- Logical Observation Identifiers Names and Codes (LOINC) for laboratory tests, vital signs and cancer case reporting; and
- CVX for immunizations.

Additionally, other vocabulary and terminology standards are embedded within implementation guides, documenting the use of data formats such as HL7 v2 messages and C-CDA. In many cases, "value sets," such as those published in the Value Set Authority Center (VSAC), are established to identify subsets of the standard vocabularies to be used for a specific purpose. For example, for the purposes of quality measurement, a unique identifier or object identifier (OID) is used to call out a grouping of codes from SNOMED CT that should be used to identify diabetic patients for diabetes quality measures. That content can be pulled through an API into a system and automatically be updated as the content is refined. The codes listed in association with the OID then determine which patients should be included or excluded from the measure based on the coding of the diabetes diagnosis, despite having been entered for the purpose of direct clinical care or billing.

Moving Forward and Milestones

Consistent and shared ways to represent the meaning of clinical concepts and terminology are necessary to support clinical care, research, quality measurement and clinical decision support. This shift will allow machines to automatically update content, understand and interpret meaning and integrate multiple coded concepts together to create more complex concepts and inferences. This will require data stewards, information science professionals and others to work together with the National Library of Medicine (NLM) to clearly represent these concepts and their relationships, as well as the mechanisms by which automated processing of such data can occur. Furthermore, the industry should increasingly embrace and build to the concept of utilizing service calls to access the most up-to-date standards, vocabularies, data elements and artifacts, rather than trying to encode each update locally in their system and treating them as static in the interim.

Near-term work to advance semantic interoperability should focus on priority data domains that are most commonly used across many clinical and non-clinical use cases and most often represented in format standards (see Figure 7). These data domains have a number of data elements included in them. The industry should prioritize which data elements should be focused on first for semantic interoperability as well as their consistent use across multiple standards. Advancing the semantic interoperability of these overarching data domains and their consistent usage in different format standards will enable data to be collected once and used for many purposes. This will also create efficiencies in electronic health information sharing that have yet to materialize across the health IT ecosystem. In the near term, this means aligning vocabularies, code sets, value sets and "null flavors" for these data domains across the most commonly used format standards, including HL7 V2 messaging, C-CDA, QRDA, NCPDP SCRIPT and HL7's Fast Healthcare Interoperability Resources (FHIR).[66] Over time, the priority data domains will be expanded to include additional clinical data. This will need to include imaging reports, genomic data and unstructured data, which would comprise of the notes and narrative that are needed to support clinical care, quality measurement, research and many other use cases.

- Individual Name
- Sex
- Date of Birth
- Race
- Ethnicity
- Address (Current, Historical)
- Phone Number (Current, Historical)
- Preferred Language
- Smoking Status
- Problems
- Medications
- Medication Allergies
- Laboratory Test(s)
- Laboratory Value(s)/Result(s)
- Vital Signs
- Procedures
- Care Team Members
- Immunizations
- Unique Device Identifier(s) for Implantable Device(s)
- Assessment and Plan of Treatment
- Goals
- Health Concerns

Figure 7. Near-term Priority Data Domains.

Overall, improvements in the consistent use and specificity of semantic representations of data will help advance and support new modes of information exchange, specifically those where stakeholders will be able to selectively request or access only the information they need (compared to the predominant document-based exchange used today). While information may still be sent as a point-in-time snapshot of a person's encounter or condition, it will increasingly be an answer to a specific, value-driven question or query. For example, while the pharmacist may request a person's current medications and allergies, their endocrinologist will likely request blood sugars, hormone levels, eye exams and the individual's person-centered plan and thus each user will receive only the information they ask for or deem relevant.

The following includes milestones for Consistent Data Semantics. Please see the Complete Set of Calls to Action and Commitments by Roadmap Section at the end of this document for the critical actions that need to take place to advance nationwide interoperability.

Milestones for Consistent Data Semantics

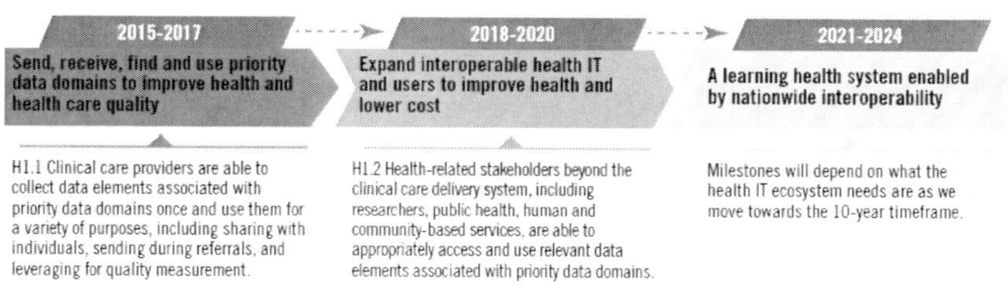

I. Consistent Data Formats

Consistently representing electronic health information across different stakeholders and systems is the bedrock of successful interoperability. In a learning health system, while user interfaces can and should be different depending on the user, the format in which electronic health information is shared between health IT systems must be consistent and machine readable, so that the meaning and integrity of information is retained as a variety of users interact with it.

Background and Current State

In the same way goods are packaged before being shipped, standardized electronic health information formats direct how electronic health information is packaged or structured so that one system can "unpack" and act upon the information that is sent by another system and vice versa. When a computer system receives electronic health information from another system, it needs to be able to process the information automatically, without time-consuming human intervention. This can only occur if the sending system has used a consistent electronic health information format that is known to, and expected by, the receiving system. Given the number of different health IT systems that must exchange electronic health information, it would be virtually impossible and grossly inefficient for each system to negotiate agreed-upon exchange formats with every other system with which it interacts. The most practical solution is for all systems to follow the same format standards when exchanging electronic health information, so that sending and receiving systems and their respective users will be able to correctly interpret, integrate, and act upon information from other systems.

Several format standards have been adopted by the Secretary in regulation as part of 2015 Edition.[67] This includes, but is not limited to:

- Consolidated Clinical Document Architecture (C-CDA)
- HL7 v2 messaging
- NCPDP SCRIPT

Various information models and representations of data are used and directly referenced by format and semantic standards today. These models provide a technically specified representation of data that engineers and developers can interpret, use and ultimately implement. The complexity of having multiple formats, vocabularies and information models makes interoperability in health IT much more challenging than other industries (e.g., ATMs, credit card processing and airline reservation systems). Harmonization of these formats and models will facilitate interoperability by reducing the effort to convert data from one format or vocabulary to another.

Another major barrier to interoperability is the approach to standards development in which individual standards pieces are built to solve a particular part of a challenge, but require implementers to put together multiple standards to fully solve the whole challenge. Often, international health IT standards are designed to satisfy many different requirements and leave the technology developer with significant choices on how to implement pieces of a standard. A solution to such problems is to build a framework of related standards that begins with a more relaxed structure, then progressively introduces levels of constraint and specificity.

Moving Forward and Milestones

Over time and for rapid innovation to take place within a learning health system, health IT stakeholders, particularly SDOs and technology developers, will need to converge and agree on the use of shared and complementary format and vocabulary standards to satisfy specific interoperability needs. The use of multiple, divergent information formats over the long term is unsustainable and perpetuates systemic roadblocks and expenses that could otherwise be removed for technology developers, providers and individuals. Format standards should continue to define and accommodate the exchange of structured and unstructured electronic health information. However, technology developers and users should design and subsequently implement systems with a very intentional movement and bias toward increased coding and exchange of more structured, standardized and discrete information. This should be accomplished while still allowing the user interface to vary so that the type of data entry and interaction is most appropriate to the user.

Despite the promise and value of structured data, the richness of unstructured documentation should not be disregarded. Without a cohesive narrative, the context of structured data can be lost. Standards should use metadata where possible to allow human users to communicate this context along with pieces of structured data. As the health IT ecosystem pulls structured information out of unstructured narrative to support a variety of analyses and user needs, a format for such metadata context will prevent information loss that can hamper the completeness clinicians and others need for sophisticated decision-making.

It is impossible for a single standard to support all the needs of a learning health system. However, every effort should be made to minimize not only the number of format standards but also to have agreement on the building blocks of these standards, the interoperability needs that each format can be used to meet (driven by a balance of local needs and national priorities) and their relationship to one another both in the standards space and in real world implementations. The already complex use of format standards in health IT will be made even more challenging when human services, genomic, patient generated health data, environmental sciences and other forms of information are integrated across the learning health system. Initiatives such as the National Information Exchange Model (NIEM)[68] should be explored as tools that may support cross-domain interoperability (see the Supplemental Materials document for more background on NIEM).

Over the next six to 10 years, SDOs and their stakeholders will need to continue to refine, align and develop standards for reusable data elements that can be used for any purpose, from documents to research to quality reporting. FHIR is one effort that is evolving and is exploring ways to accommodate alternative methods of integrating data for the specific purpose of information exchange. SDOs and technology developers should develop FHIR and/or other standards, with the impact of and requirements for a transition between standards or versions of standards as a major consideration. New standards, updates or extensions to existing standards should undergo testing in more comprehensive implementations than is typically done in the current environment, to ensure backward and forward compatibility (where possible), and SDOs should provide endorsed mappings across content and release notes across versions.

Additionally, SDOs will need to align semantic standards (vocabulary, code set, value set, and structure where applicable) for data elements associated with the priority data domains across various format standards. In some cases that will require updating format standards and/or implementation guidance to effectively accommodate data element details, such as inclusion of usable period metadata for address and telephone number in CCDA, so that technology developers and users can account for current and historical aspects of these elements to support more accurate individual data matching. Alignment efforts should start with formats and semantic standards for priority data domains and associated data elements already defined in ONC's 2015 Edition final rule.[69] Once format standards are consistently aligned for those data domains and associated elements, SDOs and stakeholders will need to agree on common semantic standards for remaining data domains and elements and align their respective format standards accordingly.

The following includes milestones for Consistent Data Formats. Please see the Complete Set of Calls to Action and Commitments by Roadmap Section at the end of this document for the critical actions that need to take place to advance nationwide interoperability.

Milestones for Consistent Data Formats

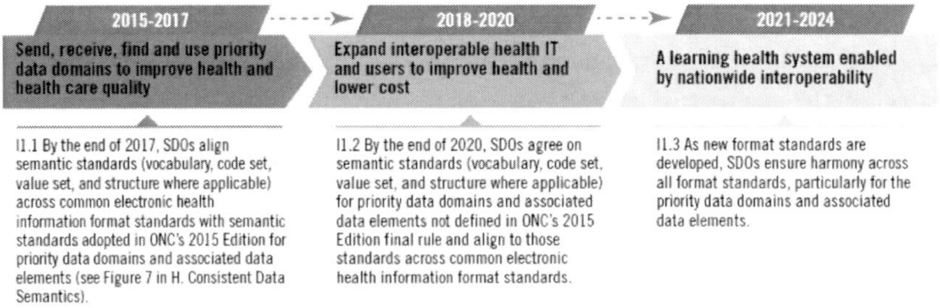

J. Secure, Standard Services

Services should be modular, secure and standards-based wherever possible.

Background and Current State

Secure, standard services that support functional capabilities are critical to successful interoperability. Currently, the secure services permitted by CMS' Meaningful Use Stage 2 requirements include Direct secure messaging, SOAP- based exchange and exchange (through a participant in the eHealth Exchange).[70] Moving forward, the ONC's Data Access Framework initiative (DAF) is evolving existing IHE and HL7 standards to support next-generation query services. The adoption of a service-oriented architecture (SOA) is fundamental to using standard services for interoperability. The concept of SOA is not new; for years, software developers have created systems with application programming interfaces (APIs) that define how systems and subsystems interact with one another by exchanging data in reliable, structured ways, and this approach is expected to be an ongoing adjunct in health IT interoperability for the foreseeable future.

All of the core services that are used to operate the Internet began as API functions. Many of these core services and APIs eventually developed into internationally recognized, open standards. In a SOA, complex systems are made available to other systems on a network and perform specific tasks. These services form system building blocks, capable of being reused over and over again in the context of different needs and applications. Diverse systems can share algorithms, features and capabilities by relying on these shared services rather than reproducing this functionality each time it is needed. Users do not need to know or be concerned about the existence of a SOA within the systems they are using. Using a SOA can dramatically reduce the cost and complexity of building and adapting systems to changing needs and environments.

One of the guiding principles for this Roadmap is the notion of *modularity*: complex systems are more durable under changing circumstances when they are divided into independent components that can be connected together. SOA is at the core of the modularity required for nationwide interoperability. But in order for interoperability to function on a wide scale, the APIs (which represent the points of contact, or boundaries, between disparate systems) need to be consistent and standardized as much as possible. Such "loose coupling" means that not all systems within organizations need to perform the same functions identically (or at all), only that when they choose to request access to information or services from each other they can communicate. Further, they should do so in predictable ways agreed upon by learning health system participants.

While many systems are proprietary in nature, some technology developers publish their API specifications to enable other systems to be interoperable with them. This publication of APIs reduces complexity by describing functions and data elements that need to be used to communicate with other health IT systems. At the scale at which a learning health system will operate, however, simply publishing APIs is not enough; there must also be a limited number of standard APIs to reduce complexity.[71] It may also be possible to utilize tools to help users navigate through some of the complexity or to modularize API requirements to allow systems to build much smaller interfaces for specific needs.

In some industries where information exchange environments are less complex, simply publishing APIs has led to enough market standardization to enable interoperability. In more complex industries, assertive, top-down coordination has been needed. However, in the complex environment of health and health care, technology developers have not always prioritized making APIs available that can be broadly and easily used to achieve core interoperability use cases and fuel innovative, market-led interoperability.

Moving Forward and Milestones

The services envisioned in this Roadmap are consistent with the vision of the JASON Report, *A Robust Health Data Infrastructure*, released in April 2014.[72] The Roadmap also considers the recommendations of the HIT Policy Committee JASON Task Force.

While it may take several years to achieve, a learning health system must converge on a limited set of standard APIs to support a core set of services that enable electronic health information to flow when and where it is needed. In the near term, it is critical for SDOs and technology developers to implement and make available standard APIs for the basic functions of querying and retrieving priority data elements as unique pieces of information and assembled into a clinical document. Future standards and APIs should be determined by a balance of user needs and nationwide health priorities. Prioritization of needs and associated work should be done through a transparent, inclusive shared decision making process (see Shared-Decision Making, Rules of Engagement and Accountability to Enable Interoperability for more detail).

The following includes milestones for Secure, Standard Services. Please see the Complete Set of Calls to Action and Commitments by Roadmap Section at the end of this document for the critical actions that need to take place to advance nationwide interoperability.

Milestones for Secure, Standard Services

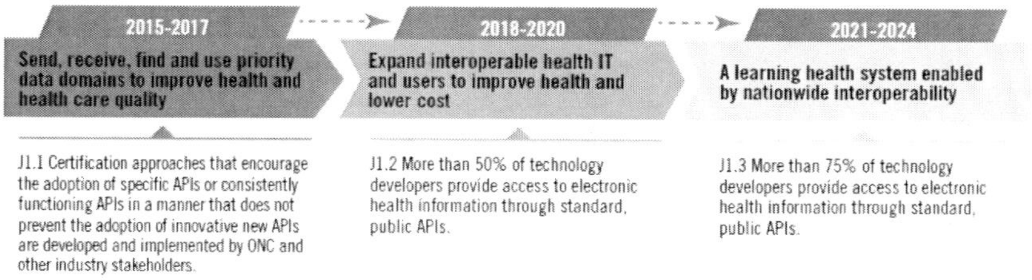

K. Consistent, Secure Transport Techniques

Interoperability requires transport techniques that are non-proprietary, easy to configure and widely and consistently used. The fewest number of protocols necessary to fulfill the needs of learning health system participants is most desirable.

Background and Current State

Transport techniques are the means by which data gets from one place to another. Transport techniques are data agnostic, meaning the content of what is being sent should be irrelevant to the operation of the transport protocol. Interoperability requires transport techniques that are non-proprietary, easy to configure and widely adopted. Security techniques such as the encryption of information in transit and assurance that electronic health information only goes to the intended recipient (individual or system) are of prime concern.

There are currently several transport techniques widely adopted across the health IT ecosystem today. ONC's 2014 and 2015 Editions' certification requirements, the Medicare and Medicaid EHR Incentive Program's requirements, and ONC's State HIE Program all encouraged or required the Direct transport protocol (commonly called Direct) to be used for exchanging electronic health information. Direct was created to lower the barriers to exchange by creating a specification that used existing email transport protocols in a secure way. While the implementation of Direct is fairly straightforward technically, it also requires trust to be established between service providers and trading partners, which has posed challenges to its widespread use.

Another commonly used transport technique today is web services. Documentation or profiles from Integrating the Healthcare Enterprise (IHE) often use Simple Object Access Protocol (SOAP)-based web services to support transport for queries, as well as services like public health reporting. The eHealth Exchange also uses SOAP-based web services in its implementation. This approach is also currently deployed by many EHR developers as it allows XML-based, system-to-system transactions to be constructed easily. Another type of web service approach includes RESTful implementations, which are growing in interest as they are leveraged by HL7's Fast Healthcare Interoperability Resources (FHIR) project.

Moving Forward and Milestones

A suite of transport standards will continue to be developed and maintained to support various nationwide interoperability needs. As with semantic and format standards, it is unlikely that just one transport standard will support all needs across a learning health system; however, the suite of transport standards adopted by learning health system participants should represent the fewest number of protocols necessary to fulfill their needs and should be consistent with core Internet technologies that are pervasively deployed.

Direct, as a transport standard for sending and receiving information between known parties, will be one important standard in this suite. Learning health system participants should continue to adopt and use Direct for simple send/receive transactions, which it supports well, and trust communities that enable Direct services to scale should (1) continue to focus on scaling trust across implementations of the specification, and (2) work to establish trust across communities such that electronic health information can flow across Direct service providers without having to be a member of multiple trust communities and as commensurate with organizations' required Level of Assurance.

Web services based on SOAP and RESTful approaches for more automated transactions, including query/response and some publish/subscribe transactions, will also be important standards in this suite. Where technology developers have SOAP-based implementations that work well,[73] they should continue to leverage those investments, while exploring RESTful transport approaches that may scale more easily and nimbly over time.

The following includes milestones for Consistent, Secure Transport Techniques. Please see the Complete Set of Calls to Action and Commitments by Roadmap Section at the end of this document for the critical actions that need to take place to advance nationwide interoperability.

Milestones for Consistent, Secure Transport Techniques

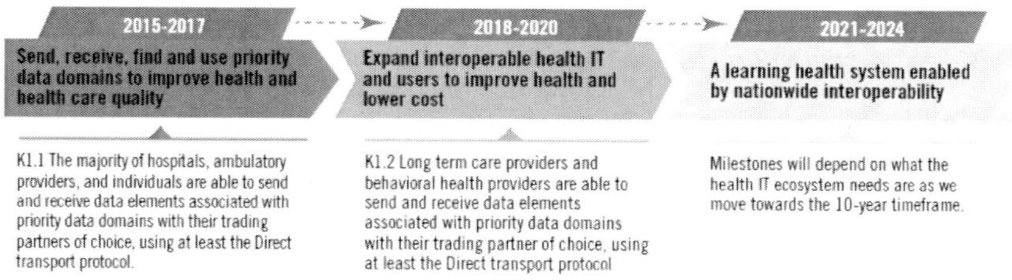

L. Accurate Individual Data Matching

Whether aggregated in a repository or linked "just in time," electronic health information from disparate sources must be accurately matched to prevent information fragmentation and the incorrect merging of records. As technology evolves, provider identities, system identities, device identities and others that support public health and clinical research will need to be accurately matched.

Background and Current State

Interoperability at a fundamental level requires the matching and linking of individuals' electronic health information across organizations. Individuals' electronic health information is often stored in multiple systems, even within a single organization. Inaccurate data matching poses a significant risk to patient safety because information may be unavailable when needed or records may be merged incorrectly, leading to inappropriate treatment choices. Errors in individual data matching will be compounded with the expansion of electronic health information sharing, as the learning health system continues to evolve and include more than individual or patient-specific information. Additional information will be matched and linked, including provider identities, system identities, device identities and others to support functions like public health and clinical research. Therefore, the nation should strive to consistently achieve 100 percent matching accuracy for electronic health information within or across organizations. To that end, improvements need to be made in the consistency and quality of data used for matching, matching processes and technology.

Unique Identifiers

While HIPAA required the creation of national identifiers for patients, providers, hospitals and payers in 1996, subsequent annual appropriations legislation has prohibited HHS from funding the promulgation or adoption of a national unique patient identifier.[74] However, the legislation does not impose a federal bar against HIEs, states, private corporations or other non-HHS government agencies from developing their own individual identification strategies and unique identifiers. In fact, many HIEs assign and use a unique identifier within their system for matching purposes. Additionally, the Department of Veterans Affairs and the Department of Defense assign a single lifetime personal identifier that follows a service member from enlistment until death. While organizations use a unique identifier within their own systems, these identifiers are typically not used amongst unaffiliated organizations to identify and match an individual's data. Individual demographics and sophisticated matching algorithms are currently the primary method for electronically matching individual data.

Matching Attributes, Data Quality and Data Integrity

In 2014, ONC released an environmental scan on individual data matching that included health systems, HER developers, health information exchange developers and master patient index developers.[75] The report found that data quality was identified by nearly all participants as a key barrier to accurate individual data matching. Individual data matching for clinical care has primarily relied on the use of data points (known as demographics), such as name, date of birth, address and others that identify individuals as uniquely as possible in combination with matching processes, which include algorithms. Consequently, the quality of individual demographic data has a significant impact on matching accuracy. At least one study found that the majority of identification errors in emergency departments could be traced back to individual demographic data being incorrectly entered during the registration process.[76] For decades, health care systems have managed this function internally with health information management professionals dedicated to laborious and costly manual clean-up. This level of effort is not efficient, sustainable or timely enough for large-scale interoperability.[77]

As noted earlier, individual data matching uses technologies such as master or community person indexes and deterministic and probabilistic matching algorithms in conjunction with individual demographics. (For more information please see the Supplemental Materials document.) However, due to widespread variability in the use and availability of matching algorithms, it is difficult to adequately compare algorithm performance across organizations. There is also no unilateral agreement across the health IT ecosystem regarding which matching methods work the best.

Measuring Match Performance

Measuring algorithm performance and overall matching accuracy is important in order to identify where and how to make improvements. Since universal performance metrics are not widely adopted, there is little agreement across the ecosystem on what should be measured near-term. The 2014 *Patient Identification and Matching Final Report* found that few organizations had insight into how well they are performing on individual data matching, with very few able to report false positive and false negative rates and in fact, disagreement amongst the organizations on what should be measured in matching.[78]

Moving Forward and Milestones

All interoperability functions depend on highly accurate methods for individual data matching, and as noted above, there are significant patient safety implications of both false positive and false negative matches. To increase the accuracy of individual data matching, a core set of individual demographic attributes should be tightly standardized, those attributes should be consistently shared during exchange transactions so they can be used for matching purposes, and best practices should be defined for improving data quality, matching processes and assessing matching performance to support improvement efforts.

A vast majority of stakeholders have called for the standardization of primary and secondary data elements, adoption of a uniform data capture methodology and standardization of performance metrics. The 2014 individual data matching report identified an initial list of data elements that should be included in exchange transactions in a standardized, consistently formatted manner. The data elements (Figure 8) were recommended in 2011 by the HIT Standards Committee and expanded based on stakeholder feedback gathered during the environmental scan.

Accurate collection of demographic attributes during the registration process is the first and potentially the most important contributor to matching accuracy by downstream and external systems. In 2013, ONC released the SAFER guide[79] that included best practices for recording demographic data. The industry should continue to build upon the SAFER guide and other efforts to document best practices that will improve data quality at the point of registration.

Due to the variability in use and availability of algorithms, there is still work to be done to determine how to appropriately measure their performance. There is some agreement in the field that currently, the best available indicator to measure matching performance is the duplicate record rate. Although the duplicate record rate is only one aspect of overall matching performance, it serves as a measurement starting point because it is widely used and one of the most accessible types of reports from current systems. Studies have found that the national average for duplicate record rates range from eight to 12 percent[80] with some very successful organizations reaching five percent.

The following includes milestones for Accurate Individual Data Matching Please see the Complete Set of Calls to Action and Commitments by Roadmap Section at the end of this document for the critical actions that need to take place to advance nationwide interoperability.

Milestones for Accurate Individual Data Matching

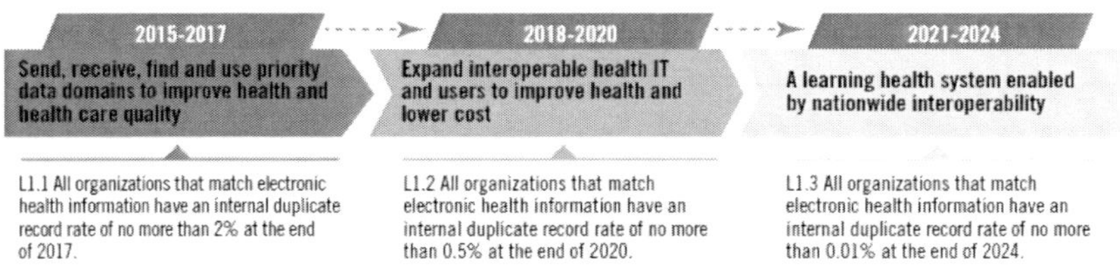

- First/Given Name
- Last/Family Name
- Previous Name
- Middle/Second Given Name (includes Middle Initial)
- Suffix
- Date of Birth
- Sex
- Address (current and historical)
- Phone Number (current and historical)

Figure 8. Data Elements for Individual Data Matching.

M. Health Care Directories and Resource Location

The ability to rapidly locate resources, including providers, individuals, APIs, networks, etc. by their current or historical names and descriptions will be necessary for finding, accessing and/or sharing electronic health information.

Background and Current State

Resource location is the electronic means for dynamically discovering participants of interest and the resources or services they offer for sharing or accessing data (including the discovery of electronic endpoints such as APIs and services such as master patient indexes). As nationwide interoperability and a learning health system advance, they will include a complex and expanding ecosystem of participants and services, and the technical standards supporting those services will evolve over time. Directories, starting with health care directories that provide resource location services, must support a wide range of exchange and data access types. These include searching for a known provider's Direct address so a summary of care can be sent, to searching for the electronic service information of all participants that support patient discovery. Health care directories also support queries for electronic health information to locate critical information about an individual (note that this includes use cases when sources of critical information are unknown before searching). Resource location is therefore a core functional requirement to support nationwide interoperability.

Efforts to advance resource location services span many years and have focused largely on the development of directories to support electronic health information sharing arrangements. A significant amount of work has been done on technical standards to support directories (see Supplemental Materials document for more history on directory standards). Some directories exist today, which are focused only on health care providers and related information such as Direct addresses (so-called "Direct White Pages"). These directories are typically contained within a particular technology developer and are not electronically shared with other technology developers or systems. The directory assets that exist today can provide a foundation for advancing broader resource location services in the near term. Many HIEs, HISPs, EHR systems, Managed Care Organizations and credentialing services operating today have some form of directory that helps identify and locate clinical and other care providers. Several state Medicaid agencies are also building provider directories. These directories can serve as the basis for the next generation of directory services.

There are also nationwide directories available that are expanding their services and may prove to be important supports for resource location services. For example, the Surescripts physician directory contains information to support electronic exchange for more than 160,000 providers,[81] and CMS maintains the National Plan and Provider Enumeration System (NPPES), which contains information for more than 4.2 million health care providers and organizations.[82] Now more than ever, NPPES is being analyzed by the health industry as a tool to support many uses.[83] One of the greatest challenges to using NPPES to support resource location services relates to business processes mentioned above: key information within NPPES, such as provider's practice addresses, telephone numbers and licensure information may be inaccurate or out-of-date because providers have little incentive to update their records. However, CMS is working to enhance the accessibility, usability and data quality of the NPPES, as illustrated in Figure 9.[84]

Moving Forward and Milestones

A learning health system will grow and change dramatically throughout its lifetime – adding new participants and changing organizational relationships; adding new services; upgrading or retiring legacy services in favor of new and evolving standards; adding new functions, APIs and stakeholders. It is unrealistic to expect any organization to keep track of all of the services available and API details for each one, even if limited to only those participants and services of interest to them. Therefore, the future architecture of resource location will almost certainly be federated and solutions pursued by the health IT ecosystem need to be flexible to support this.

Due to its dynamic nature, resource location will also have some degree of decentralized administration in order to operate efficiently and remain accurate and up-to-date. This vision of a federated and decentralized ecosystem for resource location has many positive implications. For example, if health plan directories are standardized and able to be queried by EHR directories, referrals and care coordination could be accomplished more efficiently. Standardization also supports attribution of providers to patients or providers to practices as required for new payment models. This future state could also allow for health care directories to update one another with the most recent and accurate information. Health plans that publish standardized directories could make it easier for technology developers to create tools for consumers to more easily find providers and potentially communicate with them.

- **Expanding Relevant Data:** Inclusion of additional optional information such as Direct addresses, web address and multiple practice locations.
- **Expanding Data Accessibility:** Creation of RESTful web services (APIs) for accessing public information that will allow system to system connectivity and make NPPES data easier to use by both the public and HHS/CMS.
- **Review and Notification:** Regular review and comparison of information against other available records and then notification to providers to verify the information on file to ensure accuracy.
- **Delegation of Authority:** Enabling others who have been given permission to update and manage NPPES records on a provider's behalf.
- **Reduce Duplicate Data Entry:** Allowing for two-way sharing of data between NPPES and other CMS systems such as PECOS, the provider enrollment system for Medicare.

Figure 9. Goals of the current CMS NPPES project.

In addition, a dialogue should be started that is broadly inclusive of learning health system participants to gain consensus on answers to the following critical questions:

1. How does an individual or system place a query to discover participants of a learning health system or the services they offer? How is API information passed back? How does one know that the response is complete?
2. How does an individual or system gain access to resource location services? How is one authenticated to access directories or resource location services?
3. How is information in resource location services managed and updated and how is the information curated to ensure accuracy?
4. How does an individual or system find information regarding the relationships between organizations and providers?
5. How does an individual or system find information regarding when an organization changes its name, merges with another organization or establishes additional locations?

Answers to these questions will help define an architecture for resource location, identify the technical standards that will be used to implement it and the security model to protect potentially sensitive information and determine the extent to which current directory assets can be leveraged in the future. The resources that need to be coordinated by resource location services include at least the mechanisms to locate and access data repositories, networks, services, and APIs.

The following includes milestones for Health Care Directories for Resource Location. Please see the Complete Set of Calls to Action and Commitments by Roadmap Section at the end of this document for the critical actions that need to take place to advance nationwide interoperability.

Milestones for Health Care Directories and Resource Location

Outcomes

N. Individuals Have Access to Longitudinal Electronic Health Information, Can Contribute to that Information, and Can Direct It to Any Electronic Location

Background and Current State

Individuals' ability to manage their health through access to and use of their electronic health information, and to contribute electronic health information about themselves to care providers and others is a cornerstone of efforts to support individual and family engagement in health management and improve health outcomes. Individuals often do not have easy access to their health records, despite a right to them under HIPAA, where it applies.[85] To obtain paper copies, individuals often have to face the inconvenience of going to a medical records department in person, signing forms, paying a fee and waiting 30 to 60 days to obtain their own health information.

Over the last few years, policy changes have been put in place to increase individuals' access to their electronic health information, and, increasingly, many are taking advantage of this access. In 2013 almost half of individuals given access to their clinical electronic health information online viewed it at least once within the previous year. Three quarters of those individuals who did access their electronic health information online used it to monitor their health, and four in ten shared their electronic health information with someone else.[86] However, challenges persist for many individuals to access electronic health information, including but not limited to those in underserved communities, partly due to disparities in technology access and digital and health literacy. Further, individuals' behavioral health information, social and community service information and the health information of individuals residing in long-term, post-acute care settings are still often unavailable electronically.

Though individuals are receiving increased electronic access to some clinical health information, longitudinal electronic health information is often spread across multiple providers using disparate IT systems, which makes it cumbersome for individuals to collect, share and/or use their longitudinal electronic health information from multiple sources. A number of initiatives have been implemented over the last few years to help individuals access and use their electronic health information, particularly their electronic health information, including:

- Meaningful Use Stage 2 patient and family engagement measures;
- ONC's Blue Button initiative;
- the Investing in Innovation (i2) program; and
- coordinated work on policies and technology to support patient-generated health data and person-centered care.[87]

Moving Forward and Milestones

While the concept of "patient-centered health care" has been evolving over the past decade, there is a vast distance between that concept and a truly "person-centric" vision that embraces the value of the individual inside and outside the health care system for improving both health and care. The person-centric vision is that, "the power of each individual is developed and unleashed to be active in managing their health and partnering in their health care, enabled by information and technology."[88]

Changing the paradigm to a person-centered ecosystem is vital to improving health, given that an individual's actions inside and outside the clinical care delivery system greatly impact health outcomes. Moving forward, the health IT ecosystem needs to put greater focus on (1) incorporating patient-generated health data across health IT products and services, and (2) ensuring the availability of tools for individuals to use a broad range of longitudinal electronic health information to manage their health and make more informed health-related decisions. The volume of health- related services provided in home and community-based settings is already increasing and is expected to grow over time.[89] Information from these services and care settings, along with patient-generated health data will need to be incorporated or connected with institutionally-based clinical information in timely and useful ways. Providers, government, payers and technology developers all have a role in supporting and empowering individuals to become effective managers of their health and wellness where they live, work and play, using information and technology.

The following includes milestones for individuals to have access to longitudinal electronic health information, contribute to that information, and direct it to any electronic location. Please see the Complete Set of Calls to Action and Commitments by Roadmap Section at the end of this document for the critical actions that need to take place to advance nationwide interoperability.

Milestones for Individuals have access to longitudinal electronic health information, can contribute to that information, and can direct it to any electronic location

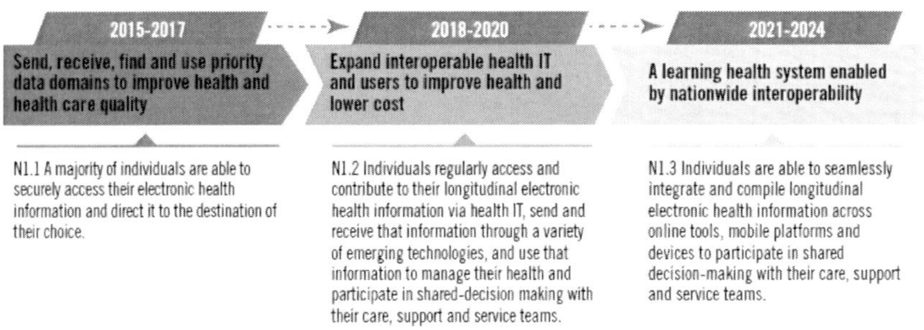

O. Provider Workflows and Practices Include Consistent Sharing and Use of Patient Information from All Available and Relevant Sources

Background and Current State

Providers[90] are critical to delivery system reform and the transformation to a learning health system. Rigorous training, continuing education and maintenance of certification programs, coupled with decades of advancement and innovation in health care have earned providers the trust of the American public. Most importantly, the profound and fundamental nature of the patient-provider relationship sets the profession of medicine apart from most others and has earned its practitioners the honor of participating in many of the most important events and decisions that individuals and families face.

In partnership with individuals, their families and caregivers, health care providers and provider organizations are central to the delivery of high quality, safe and efficient health care. Providers jointly make decisions with individuals about diagnosis and treatment and play a critical role in providing information to individuals while also coordinating care with other providers. As stewards of the majority of clinical health information today, it is important that information be electronically shared in a timely manner with individuals, their authorized representative(s) and other care team members. Many provider communities have recognized that team-based care, strong care coordination and effective patient engagement are fundamental to an efficient and effective care delivery system.

Providers also play a critical role in coordinating care with other providers in support of patients. However, coordinating care and engaging with multi-disciplinary, cross-organization care, support and service teams has been incredibly difficult with the tools available today. Technology that does not facilitate the sharing and use of electronic health information that providers need, when they need it, which often creates additional challenges to care coordination. Additionally, care coordination via electronic means requires workflow changes for providers and their staff, particularly to close referral loops and ensure all of an individual's health information is available to the entire care, support and services team. These workflow changes are not insignificant and must be overcome in order to enable interoperability.

Moving Forward and Milestones

Providers should have the tools they need to support care transformation, i.e. using technology that supports the critical role of information sharing. This shift will open up new possibilities for providers in how they engage with patients and interact with other care, support and service team members.

For example, person-centered planning, which includes individual goals and preferences, is increasingly recognized as an integral tool for supporting person-centered health, individual-provider partnerships, and coordinating care, particularly for individuals with chronic conditions and multiple co-morbidities. In a learning health system, person- centered plans will be seamlessly shared amongst a group of individuals in a way that allows all care, support and service team members to contribute to and maintain the person-centered plan. These interoperable plans will be used to support informed, shared decision-making between providers, patients and the full care support team. See the Supplemental Materials document for more on current person-centered planning efforts.

In a learning health system, data will be created and collected automatically during the routine provision of care including telehealth or e-visits, alleviating the need for duplicate entry of data into registries and other parallel systems. This data will not only seamlessly enable improvement in the quality of care, but also, as enabled by individual permission, support secondary uses of data that help to achieve important advances in population health management, public health and the generation of new biomedical knowledge. Close integration of CDS into health IT systems will enable the rapid dissemination of new knowledge to support the use of best evidence in the care of all patients, especially those with multiple, complex or rare conditions. This supports providers in ensuring they have the most updated, medically-relevant information to identify the best course(s) of treatment for the individual and discuss those options with the patient.

Further, the learning health system will require nationwide interoperability to support transparent, integrated cost and quality data, accurate outcome measures, and a continuous cycle of improvement. Information gathered and decisions made during the normal course of care will be transformed, in real-time, into computable data and knowledge that is shared across the learning health system.

The following includes milestones for Provider Workflows and Practices Include Consistent Sharing and Use of Patient Information from All Available and Relevant Sources. Please see the Complete Set of Calls to Action and Commitments by Roadmap Section at the end of this document for the critical actions that need to take place to advance nationwide interoperability.

Milestones for Provider Workflows and Practices Include Consistent Sharing and Use of Patient Information From All Available and Relevant Sources

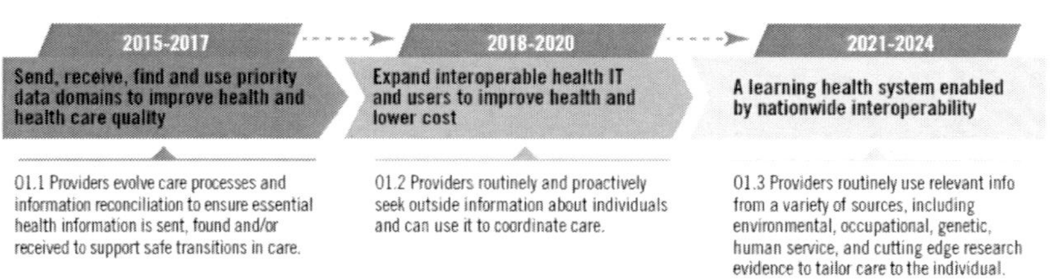

P. Tracking Progress and Measuring Success

Measuring nationwide interoperability directly informs our national progress toward achieving better care, smarter spending and healthier people and ultimately a learning health system. Our national progress on interoperability also has direct implications on the success of federal initiatives such as delivery system reform and achieving "widespread interoperability" as outlined in the Medicare Access and CHIP Reauthorization Act of 2015 (MACRA). Tracking and reporting on progress allows us to know where we are collectively starting from, how much progress we have made over time and whether we have met important milestones. Moreover, ONC and stakeholders can better assess the need to refine strategies outlined in the Roadmap and make course corrections as needed.

Core Aspects of Interoperability Measurement: Defining Success

How success is measured and defined will evolve over time. However, three key areas are critical to success and require measurement: capability to exchange electronic health information in an interoperable manner; information flow and usage of this information; and impacts that result from interoperability.

Measuring success in these areas will require developing a core set of measures designed to capture progress across the ecosystem over time. Success will also require determining whether stated milestones in the Roadmap were achieved, including identifying best practices and lessons learned.

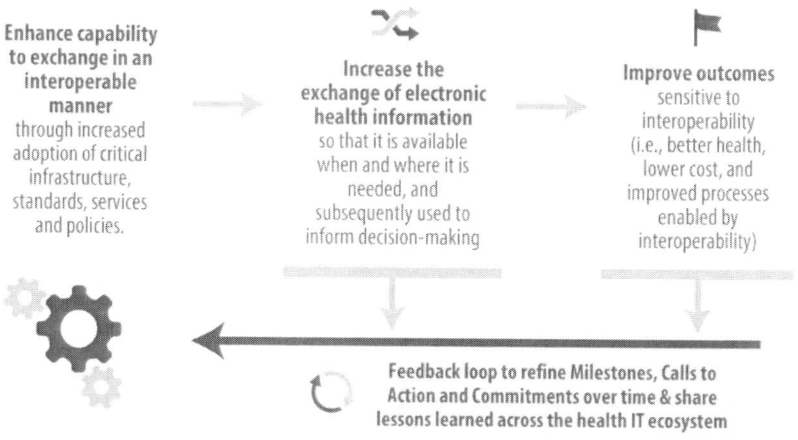

Figure 10. Framework for Assessing Nationwide Progress on Interoperability.

Measuring Success through 2017

The near-term priority is enabling individuals and providers along the care continuum (e.g. office-based physicians, hospitals, behavioral health care providers, long-term and post-acute care providers) to send, receive, find and use priority data elements. Therefore, the industry at large should initially focus its measurement efforts on assessing the extent to which the exchange and use of priority data elements is increasing and the impact this increase has on care delivery. The ease by which individuals can access their electronic health information is also important to measure. To track our collective progress in the near-term the following types of domains should be reported on:

- **Exchange of Electronic Health Information:** It is important to assess how information is moving electronically. This involves measuring the extent to which individuals and providers along the care continuum can electronically send, receive, find, and use priority data elements in an interoperable manner. For example, identifying a reduction in the amount of paper-based exchange methods (e.g., fax) could be an indication that providers and individuals are increasingly using electronic, interoperable methods to exchange data.
- **Availability of Electronic Health Information:** Electronic health information should be available to both providers and individuals when and where they need it. The availability of electronic health information from outside sources, starting with the priority data elements listed in the Roadmap, will serve as key indicators of the degree to which information is accessible and interoperable. It is also important to assess the extent to which data is made available to appropriate parties outside a health care providers' organization (e.g. patients, providers, outside organization).
- **Use of Electronic Health Information in Decision-Making:** To achieve desired clinical and health impacts, electronic health information should be used effectively. Measures in this domain will assess whether electronic health information from outside sources is used to inform decision-making and manage care. Measuring usage will enable us to understand how information from outside sources is used and valued.

Using measures identified within these core domains and progress reported on stated milestones in the Roadmap, success in the near-term is defined as:

Near-Term Success

An increase in the proportion of individuals, office-based physicians, hospitals and behavioral health, long-term care and post-acute care providers that:

- Send, receive, find and use electronic health information;
- Have electronic health information available from outside sources and make electronic health information available to outside sources; and
- Use electronic health information to inform decision-making.

Currently, ONC relies on self-reported data from national surveys and federal reporting requirements (i.e., the Medicare and Medicaid EHR Incentive Program data). The national surveys include data from office-based physicians, hospitals, individuals and a subset of providers in long-term care settings. In the near-term, ONC is limited in its measurement to these populations and data sources. Expanding the populations covered to include behavioral health care providers and the broader long-term and post-acute care community, as well as shifting to electronically generated data from certified EHR systems or other systems, will require collaboration and coordination with federal partners and stakeholders across the ecosystem.

ONC has taken a lead role in measuring and reporting on progress related to health IT adoption and use across the nation. However, assessing nationwide progress requires participation of stakeholders across entire the ecosystem. ONC, federal partners and stakeholders must work together to identify measures, data sources and barriers to interoperability.

To address near-term measurement gaps, ONC is exploring a number of opportunities. ONC seeks to collaborate with entities that enable exchange and interoperability, such as technology developers, HIOs and HISPs to develop and report on measures based on system usage. Where data sources for measurement are lacking, such as adoption and implementation of standards, ONC may also commission market reports. Additionally, ONC lacks data sources necessary to measure near-term success for long-term care and behavioral health providers. ONC will work with these communities and federal partners, such as CMS and SAMHSA, to address this gap.

Measuring Success through 2018 and Beyond

Nationwide interoperability has the potential to support a number of processes to help improve individuals' experiences with the health care delivery system, reduce costs, increase efficiency of care and improve health outcomes. It is therefore important to measure whether nationwide interoperability is having its intended affect. ONC recognizes that the current measures for assessing interoperability are necessary but not sufficient to monitor progress in the long- term. Consequently, over time, in addition to measuring the flow and use of information, there will need to be a shift to defining success in terms of outcomes.

Based on identified measures, progress on stated milestones in the Roadmap, and lessons learned in the near-term; success in the long-term is defined as:

Long-Term Success

An increase in the proportion of individuals and entities across the broader ecosystem that:

- Send, receive, find and use electronic health information;
- Have electronic health information available from outside sources and make electronic health information available to outside sources; and
- Use electronic health information to inform decision-making.

Resulting in

- Positive impacts on outcomes sensitive to interoperability (i.e., better health, lower cost and improved processes enabled by interoperability).

The Roadmap has discussed expanding health IT and its users beyond providers across the care continuum, to include non-health care settings (i.e., schools, social services) and public health. ONC must work with federal partners and key stakeholders to identify data sources and potential measures that will reflect how this broader ecosystem shares electronic health-related information.

Stakeholder involvement will be critical to identifying key outcomes sensitive to interoperability. HHS plans to support the development of measures focused on the impacts of interoperable exchange through organizations such as the National Quality Forum (NQF). Moreover, developing measures related to how nationwide interoperability supports learning health systems will involve engaging organizations such as research consortiums, federal agencies and organizations involved with supporting research and the research community.

The following includes milestones for Measuring Success. Please see the Complete Set of Calls to Action and Commitments by Roadmap Section at the end of this document for the critical actions that need to take place to advance nationwide interoperability.

Milestones, Calls to Action and Commitments for Measuring Success

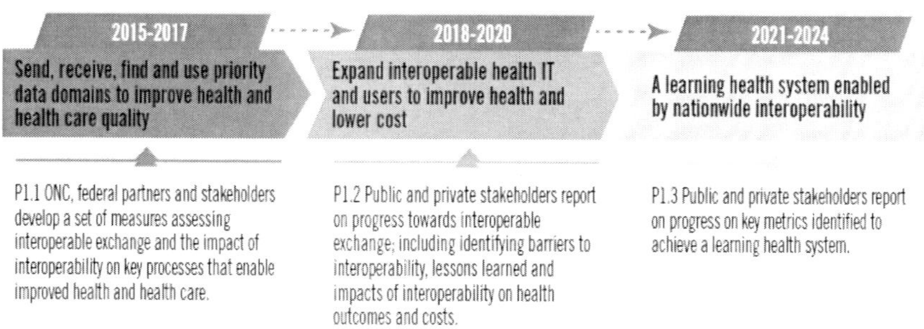

Complete Milestones, Calls to Action and Commitments

Table 1. Milestones, Calls to Action and Commitments for a Supportive Payment and Regulatory Environment

Category	2015-2017 Send, receive, find and use priority data elements to improve health and health care quality	2018-2020 Expand interoperable health IT and users to improve health and lower cost	2021-2024 Achieve nationwide interoperability to enable a learning health system
A1. Milestones	1. CMS will aim to administer 30% of all Medicare payments to providers through alternative payment models that reward quality and value, and encourage interoperability by the end of 2016.	2. CMS will administer 50% of all Medicare payments to providers through alternative payment models that reward quality and value by the end of 2018.	3. The federal government will use value-based payment models as the dominant mode of payment for providers.
A2. Calls to Action	1. All states should consider having operational plans for supporting interoperability in their health-related strategic plans. 2. States should propose and/or implement strategies to leverage Medicaid financial support for interoperability. 3. Roughly half of states should use their state-level authorities to advance interoperability beyond their current efforts. 4. States with managed care contracts should routinely require provider networks to report performance on measures of standards-based exchange of information in required quality strategies, performance measurement reporting, etc.	8. States should encourage health information exchange usage as part of Managed Care Contract (MCO) Request for Proposal (RFP) and contracts and use other state-level authorities to support interoperability, 9. Public and private payers should be unified around a common approach to administering value-based models. 10. The federal government should reinforce safe transitions of care facilitated by the timely electronic exchange of necessary, standardized clinical data through Medicare requirements. 11. A significant portion of active federal grants and contracts that include provisions related to health IT	15. All purchasers and health plans, including states and the federal government, should consistently include requirements around health IT adoption and health information exchange use in their contracted networks, when applicable. 16. The federal government should use Medicare requirements to recognize use of interoperable health IT and standards-based exchange consistent with clinical and safety statutory requirements. 17. All states may be encouraged to use initiatives around value-based arrangements under Medicaid to provide electronic tools to improve care coordination and

Category	2015-2017 Send, receive, find and use priority data elements to improve health and health care quality	2018-2020 Expand interoperable health IT and users to improve health and lower cost	2021-2024 Achieve nationwide interoperability to enable a learning health system
	5. A growing number of private payers should implement provisions supporting interoperability within value-based payment arrangements covering commercial populations. 6. Purchasers should consider health plans' commitment to the use of interoperable health IT and health information exchange among network and non-network providers in their purchasing decisions. 7. ONC should work with CMS to evaluate the use of health IT by providers participating in advanced payment models.	adoption and exchange align with national standards for health IT. 12. States with managed care contracts should increasingly require adoption and use of interoperable health IT and health information exchange. 13. The vast majority of states should use state-level authorities to support interoperability. 14. Private and public payers should align on common performance measures for interoperability and exchange for incorporation into value-based models.	deliver quality improvement data to providers.
A3. Commitments	1. CMS will take advantage of opportunities, when possible, to build interoperability requirements into relevant payment rules and programs where appropriate. 2. CMS will encourage states with Medicaid managed care programs to include references to health IT or health information exchange in any relevant sections of their state quality strategies.[91]	3. CMS will require use of certified health IT for APMs as defined by MACRA, by 2019.[92] 4. CMS will encourage states to more aggressively require HIE as part of Managed Care Contract (MCO) Request for Proposal (RFP) and contracts.	5. Access to seamless and secure patient data across the care continuum will be an expectation for providers serving beneficiaries of federal health plans.

Table 2. Milestones, Calls to Action and Commitments for Shared Decision-Making, Rules of Engagement and Accountability to Enable Interoperability

Category	2015-2017 Send, receive, find and use priority data elements to improve health and health care quality	2018-2020 Expand interoperable health IT and users to improve health and lower cost	2021-2024 Achieve nationwide interoperability to enable a learning health system
B1. Milestones	1. At least 50% of electronic health information sharing arrangements (as defined in Shared Decision-Making, Rules of Engagement and Accountability), including health information service providers (HISPs), adhere to recommended policies and business practices such that electronic health information can be exchanged by participants across organizational boundaries.	2. 100% of electronic health information sharing arrangements (as defined in Shared Decision-Making, Rules of Engagement and Accountability), including HISPs, adhere to recommended policies and business practices such that electronic health information can be exchanged by participants across organizational boundaries.	3. Non-healthcare stakeholders, such as human services, community-based services and researchers are included in electronic health information sharing arrangements in support of a learning health system.
B2. Calls to Action	1. Public and private sector health IT stakeholders should establish shared-decision making process to address operational issues related to standards, services, policies and practices that enable interoperability, including agreement on a nationwide learning health system technical architecture, and establishing clear, consistent feedback between SDOs and implementers about implementation successes and limitations, as well as supporting non-certification related testing of technical standards. 2. Participants in the shared decision making process should agree on a nationwide technical architecture for an interoperable learning health system. 3. Federal agencies that provide or pay for health services should align their policies for interoperability with ONC's policy guidance.	10. The shared decision-making process should continue to operate and update standards, services, policies and practices to enable interoperability as needed and evaluate the efficacy of standards and testing tools. 11. ONC and stakeholders participating in the shared decision-making process, human service providers and health-related device overseers should define standards, services, policies and practices for interoperability of clinical electronic health information to support research and big data.	15. The shared decision-making process should continue to operate and update standards, services, policies and practices to enable interoperability as needed and evaluate the efficacy of standards and testing tools.

<table>
<tr><th>Category</th><th>2015-2017
Send, receive, find and use priority data elements to improve health and health care quality</th><th>2018-2020
Expand interoperable health IT and users to improve health and lower cost</th><th>2021-2024
Achieve nationwide interoperability to enable a learning health system</th></tr>
<tr><td></td><td>4. Existing and future data sharing arrangements between organizations should align with ONC's policy guidance.
5. ONC, in collaboration with stakeholders, should define a policy framework for exchange of patient-generated health data and pilot it.
6. Participants in the shared decision making process should prioritize use cases based on a balance of national priorities and local needs.
7. Participants in the shared decision-making process should work with ONC to establish metrics for monitoring and assessing nationwide interoperability and methods for data collection.
8. The shared decision-making process should select standards for specific use cases/functions from ONC's most recent finalized Interoperability Standards Advisory (ISA) when the ISA contains relevant standards.
9. Health IT developers, certification programs and governing bodies should look first to ONC's most recent finalized Interoperability Standards Advisory when making decisions about the standards they will use to enable specific interoperability functions and use cases.</td><td>analyses and electronic health information from non-clinical sources
12. ONC and stakeholders should use nationwide interoperability metrics to assess the success of policy guidance and shared decision making processes to make or recommend changes, as needed.
13. The shared decision-making process should use the standards evaluation process on an ongoing basis to coordinate the roll out of software and service changes so as not to disrupt established interoperability.
14. Technology developers should give users methods by which they can electively update their technology to pilot and test new versions of standards.</td><td></td></tr>
<tr><td>B3. Commitments</td><td>1. ONC will publish an advisory that addresses policies and business practices that advance trust and interoperability.
2. ONC will annually publish and update a list of the best available standards and implementation specifications for health IT interoperability purposes and to support priority learning health system functions (ONC's Interoperability Standards Advisory (ISA)). ONC will create this ISA list through an open and transparent process that facilitates competition between standards for selection.</td><td>3. ONC will work with the established shared decision-making process to identify needs related to ONC's certification program or policy guidance.
4. ONC will continue to annually publish an updated ISA identifying the best available interoperability standards and implementation specifications.</td><td>Commitments will depend on what the health IT ecosystem needs are as we move towards the 10-year timeframe.</td></tr>
</table>

Table 3. Milestones, Calls to Action and Commitments for Ubiquitous, Secure Network Infrastructure

Category	2015-2017 Send, receive, find and use priority data elements to improve health and health care quality	2018-2020 Expand interoperable health IT and users to improve health and lower cost	2021-2024 Achieve nationwide interoperability to enable a learning health system
C1. Milestones	1. 100% of Technology developers should follow best practice guidance for "building security in" their health IT products and services. Security considerations should be incorporated at all phases of the software development lifecycle, including penetration testing. Health IT products and services should be deployed with secure defaults enabled, such as encryption, and easily patched when security issues are identified.	2. The joint public-private Cybersecurity Workgroup within Health and Public Health (HPH) continues to develop and release general cybersecurity best practices and guidance, such as tailored NIST Cybersecurity Framework, encryption, risk management, monitoring and security testing implementation guides for varying levels of audiences.	3. As a result of the efforts from the joint public-private Cybersecurity Workgroup, 80% of large organizations in the HPH sector adopt the NIST Cybersecurity Framework or equivalent risk management framework that addresses common security risks and controls such as encryption, monitoring, and security testing.
C2. Calls to Action	1. Organizations deploying health IT should ensure that it is deployed and maintained in a secure manner, including regular penetration testing and security risk assessments. 2. Health care organizations should implement the NIST Cybersecurity Framework[93] as part of their Risk Management and Incident Management programs 3. Health care organizations should participate in an information sharing environment such as an Information Sharing and Analysis Organizations (ISAO) or Information Sharing and Analysis Center (ISAC) to share and retrieve threat information in an ongoing basis. 4. Technology developers should follow Department of Homeland Security (DHS) and NIST guidance for "building security in" their health IT products and services. Security	6. As a best practice, health care providers, business associates, technology developers, and other industry stakeholders sharing electronic health information should encrypt the information "in transit" across public and private networks, except in cases where a patient requests an unencrypted communication. 7. Health IT stakeholders should develop metrics to	8. As a best practice, health care providers, business associates, technology developers, and other industry stakeholders sharing electronic health information should encrypt the information "at rest" across public and private networks, except in cases where a patient requests an unencrypted communication.

Category	2015-2017 Send, receive, find and use priority data elements to improve health and health care quality	2018-2020 Expand interoperable health IT and users to improve health and lower cost	2021-2024 Achieve nationwide interoperability to enable a learning health system
	considerations should be incorporated at all phases of the software development lifecycle, including penetration testing. 5. Health care providers, business associates, technology developers, and other industry stakeholders should begin adopting existing encryption standards to ensure that all electronic IIHI is encrypted "at rest" and "in transit," taking advantage of the most robust commercially available algorithms such as AES-256 as identified by NIST.[94] Encryption solutions should be able to be upgraded to address emerging standards without requiring a complete replacement of existing hardware.	measure and monitor progress on security risk assessments and encryption practices across the health IT ecosystem.	
C3. Commitments	1. ONC will identify best practices for implementing encryption policies for existing at rest and in transit encryption standards (e.g., NIST). 2. ONC will work with payers to explore the availability of private sector financial incentives to increase the rate of encrypting, starting with discussions with casualty insurance carriers who offer cybersecurity insurance. 3. ONC will coordinate with the Office of the Assistant Secretary for Preparedness and Response (ASPR) on priority issues related to cybersecurity for critical public health infrastructure. 4. HHS will continue to support, promote, and enhance the capability of a health and public health sector Information Sharing and Analysis Center (ISAO) for bi-directional information sharing about cyber threats and vulnerabilities between private health care industry and the federal government. 5. ONC will work with NIST and OCR to finalize and publish the NIST Critical Infrastructure Cybersecurity Framework and HIPAA Security Rule Crosswalk.	6. ONC will work with stakeholders and ASPR to develop best practices for actions that small & medium size health care organizations can take when they become aware of cyber threats. ONC will consult with OCR to make sure the practices are compliant with the HIPAA Rules.	Commitments will depend on what the health IT ecosystem needs are as we move towards the 10-year timeframe.

Table 4. Milestones, Calls to Action and Commitments for Verifiable Identity and Authentication of All Participants

Category	2015-2017 Send, receive, find and use priority data elements to improve health and health care quality	2018-2020 Expand interoperable health IT and users to improve health and lower cost	2021-2024 Achieve nationwide interoperability to enable a learning health system
D1. Milestones	1. 65% of health care organizations permit patient access to patient portals via username and password plus knowledge-based attributes or emerging technologies in lieu of passwords to reduce vulnerabilities in identity theft.	2. At least 50% of health care organizations have implemented identity proofing and authentication best practices developed in D3.1.	3. 90% of health care registration systems support the creation of accounts for caregivers, proxies and personal representatives.
D2. Calls to Action	1. Technology developers should develop or adopt innovative solutions, such as mobile technologies and RESTful approaches, to provide efficient, effective paths for individual and provider identity authentication. 2. Health care organizations should work with identity SDOs (e.g., Safebiopharma, Kantara, OpenID foundation, OAuth2) to ensure health care use cases are addressed in identity management frameworks. 3. Health care industry stakeholders should begin leveraging the Federal Identity, Credential, and Access Management (FICAM) Roadmap and Implementation Guide for identity management standards and best practices. 4. The Federal Health Architecture (FHA) and participating federal agencies should adopt ONC recommended best practices on authentication. 5. NIST, OCR, CMS, CDC, FDA and other stakeholders should collaborate regarding approaches for identity management, including HIPAA guidance for remote identity, authentication and access management.	6. Health care providers and their technical systems should allow authentication using credentials issued by other organizations by leveraging existing and evolving technologies. 7. Health care providers and their technical systems should allow authentication using credentials issued by other organizations that meet ONC best practices. 8. Health care organizations should find the right balance of security and usability by taking into consideration the diverse characteristics of their consumers 9. Health care organizations should adopt identity proofing and authentication best practices developed in D3.1.	Calls to action will depend on what the health IT ecosystem needs are as we move towards the 10-year timeframe.

Category	2015-2017 **Send, receive, find and use priority data elements to improve health and health care quality**	2018-2020 **Expand interoperable health IT and users to improve health and lower cost**	2021-2024 **Achieve nationwide interoperability to enable a learning health system**
D3. Commitments	1. ONC, in consultation with stakeholders, will establish and adopt best practices for provider and individual/consumer identity proofing and authentication, including specific levels of assurance, and will consult with OCR to ensure they are consistent with the HIPAA Security Rule and best practices already adopted for other comparable industries.	Calls to action will depend on what the health IT ecosystem needs are as we move towards the six-year timeframe.	Commitments will depend on what the health IT ecosystem needs are as we move towards the 10-year timeframe.

Table 5. Milestones, Calls to Action and Commitments for Consistent Representation of Authorization to Access Data or Services

Category	2015-2017 **Send, receive, find and use priority data elements to improve health and health care quality**	2018-2020 **Expand interoperable health IT and users to improve health and lower cost**	2021-2024 **Achieve nationwide interoperability to enable a learning health system**
E1. Milestones	1. 30% of health care organizations convey information on user attributes and authentication using agreed upon assertion technology, such as SAML, Organization for the Advancement of Structured Information Standards (OASIS) or other nationally recognized standards, when requesting electronic health information across organizational boundaries.	2. 90% or more of health care organizations convey information on user attributes and authentication using standard assertion technology.	3. Large scale adoption of authentication and authorization technology by 100% of healthcare organizations to increase and facilitate access to data.
E2. Calls to Action	1. Health care organizations and other organizations with access to electronic IIHI should ensure that their access control rules and organizational policies are aligned to leverage permitted uses and disclosure under HIPAA to advance interoperable exchange of information and the learning health system.	4. Technology developers and health care organizations should consistently implement a common standards-based approach for expressing and communicating authorization for electronic health information access/use.	Calls to action will depend on what the health IT ecosystem needs are as we move towards the 10-year timeframe.

Table 5. (Continued)

Category	2015-2017 Send, receive, find and use priority data elements to improve health and health care quality	2018-2020 Expand interoperable health IT and users to improve health and lower cost	2021-2024 Achieve nationwide interoperability to enable a learning health system
	2. Health care organizations and other organizations with access to IIHI should ensure that their access controls enable individuals or third parties designated by individuals to electronically access and transport electronic health information about that individual where the individual directs, consistent with HIPAA's patient access rules. 3. SDOs should work with technology developers to conduct pilots of standards-based approaches, including RESTful approaches, for expressing and communicating authorization for electronic health information access/use.		
E3. Commitments	1. ONC, in collaboration with stakeholders, will work to identify the technical standards and means by which a user's authority can be clearly represented among exchange partners. 2. OCR will consider where additional guidance may be needed to help stakeholders understand how HIPAA Privacy and Security Rules apply in an environment where ACOs and other multi-stakeholder entities permeate the landscape in support of value-based purchasing. 3. ONC will convene workshops or listening sessions on the types of electronic health information sharing that may be required, by role, to support value-based purchasing. A major goal of the workshops will be to evaluate how close the nation can come to achieving its interoperability goals through existing privacy rules.	4. ONC will determine next steps based on feedback from health care organizations and other stakeholders on access controls. 5. ONC will determine next steps on feedback received through workshops or listening sessions on data sharing.	6. ONC will determine next steps on feedback received through workshops or listening sessions on data sharing.

Table 6. Milestones, Calls to Action and Commitments for Consistent Understanding and Technical Representation of Permission to Collect, Share and Use Identifiable Electronic Health Information

Category	2015-2017 Send, receive, find and use priority data elements to improve health and health care quality	2018-2020 Expand interoperable health IT and users to improve health and lower cost	2021-2024 Achieve nationwide interoperability to enable a learning health system
F1. Milestones	1. The health IT ecosystem understands and promotes that in general, HIPAA enables the interoperable exchange of electronic health information for TPO without first needing to seek an individual's permission.	2. Technology developers implement technical standards and implementation guidance for consistently capturing, communicating and processing Basic Choice.	3. Technology developers implement technical standards and implementation guidance for consistently capturing, communicating and processing Granular Choice.
F2. Calls to Action	1. A majority of states should conduct an assessment of their health privacy laws to determine alignment with permitted uses of electronic health information regulated by HIPAA. 2. Professional Associations of health lawyers should educate their members about how the current HIPAA rules support interoperable exchange and patient access as important supports for national policy to improve health and build a learning health system. 3. Federal and state governments, in coordination with organizational health information privacy policymakers, should conduct outreach and disseminate educational materials about Permitted Uses and Disclosure, and Individual Access to health information. 4. ONC, standards development organizations, technology developers and appropriate stakeholders should harmonize technical standards and implementation guidance for consistently capturing, communicating and processing Basic Choice across the ecosystem.[95]	6. States that have more privacy protective laws than HIPAA should conduct a gap analysis between state privacy policy, federal law (HIPAA), and other existing laws pertaining to sensitive information and begin to develop legislative and administrative agendas to standardize these laws. 7. Technology developers and health care organizations should implement rules engines using the open source mappings for sensitive health conditions. 8. ONC, SDOs, technology developers and appropriate stakeholders should harmonize	Calls to action will depend on what the health IT ecosystem needs are as we move towards the 10-year timeframe.

Table 6. (Continued)

Category	2015-2017 Send, receive, find and use priority data elements to improve health and health care quality	2018-2020 Expand interoperable health IT and users to improve health and lower cost	2021-2024 Achieve nationwide interoperability to enable a learning health system
	5. Technology developers should begin implementing harmonized standards that document and communicate an individual's Basic Choice.	technical standards and implementation guidance for consistently capturing, communicating and processing Granular Choice across the ecosystem based on consensus categories of sensitive health information and rules for Granular Choice.	
F3. Commitments	1. ONC, in collaboration with states, national and local associations, and other federal agencies will launch a project to better understand the complexity of the rules environment, especially the diversity among more privacy restrictive state laws and their impact on computable privacy. 2. ONC will identify a definition of "Basic Choice" and provide policy guidance regarding if/when Basic Choice should be offered, even when not required by law based on recommendations from the HITPC by the end of CY 2016. 3. ONC will analyze and provide guidance on the consequences of offering Basic Choice on an Opt in vs. Opt out basis. 4. ONC will monitor other consent management work such as: the Social Security Administration's (SSA) written permission to share data across states for disability determinations, and FTC's implementation of simple consumer preferences (akin to "basic choice") through the FTC's "Do Not Call" Registry to determine lessons applicable to Basic Choice for electronic health information sharing.	9. ONC will work with State governments and other federal agencies to develop consensus categories of "sensitive" health information, particularly those regarding clinically sensitive and age-based rules. 10. ONC will work with State governments and other federal agencies to develop consensus categories of "sensitive" health information, particularly those regarding clinically sensitive and age-based rules 11. Based on industry input, ONC will provide guidance on the best technical architecture for managing individual permission	Commitments will depend on what the health IT ecosystem needs are as we move towards the 10-year timeframe.

Category	2015-2017 Send, receive, find and use priority data elements to improve health and health care quality	2018-2020 Expand interoperable health IT and users to improve health and lower cost	2021-2024 Achieve nationwide interoperability to enable a learning health system
	5. Federal government (e.g., Office for Civil Rights (OCR) and Substance Abuse and Mental Health Services Administration (SAMHSA)), will consider where additional guidance in the form of education and outreach may be needed to help stakeholders understand a) the applicability of federal regulations regarding the confidentiality of substance use information b) how the HIPAA Privacy Rule permits health information to be exchanged (use and disclosure) for TPO without permission. 6. OCR, in collaboration with ONC, will work to address barriers that prevent patients from accessing their health data. OCR will develop additional guidance materials to educate the public and health care providers about a patient's right to access his or her electronic health information under HIPAA. 7. Federal and state governments, in coordination with organizational health information privacy policymakers, will conduct outreach and disseminate educational materials about Permitted Uses and Disclosure and Individual Access to health information. 8. ONC will convene a group of industry stakeholders to determine if it is possible to create an open source mapping of the codes that capture clinical care to sensitive health conditions such as mental health. These mappings can serve as the foundation for common rules to be used by rules engines for determining what data may be shared based on individual permission.	across the health IT ecosystem that meets FIPPs (see the Supplemental Materials) and will update guidance as/if necessary.	

Table 7. Milestones, Calls to Action and Commitments for an Industry-wide Testing and Certification Infrastructure to Advance Health IT Interoperability

Category	2015-2017 Send, receive, find and use priority data elements to improve health and health care quality	2018-2020 Expand interoperable health IT and users to improve health and lower cost	2021-2024 Achieve nationwide interoperability to enable a learning health system
G1. Milestones	1. ONC and industry-led testing and certification programs develop a standard set of best practices and policies that ensure consistency across testing and certification bodies.	2. Providers are able to self-test their deployed health IT for core interoperability functions to ensure their systems operate as expected after implementation and to hold technology developers and network service providers accountable.	3. A comprehensive testing infrastructure exists for providers to continuously test their health IT as new components are added and old components are phased out to ensure their systems operate as expected after implementation and to hold technology developers and network service providers accountable.
G2. Calls to Action	1. Technology developers, SDOs, government and other stakeholders should accelerate the development and availability of a suite of testing tools that can be used by technology users, not just developers, post-implementation to test and ensure interoperability while health IT is in use. 2. SDOs should release comprehensive schema and associated testing tools for each standard and implementation guide they release in order to support more stringent testing of standards by technology developers.	5. Multiple industry-led health IT certification programs should exist to address stakeholder needs, including post-implementation testing and surveillance. 6. More than 50% of the test tools approved for use by the ONC Health IT Certification Program should be non-governmental. 7. More than 75% of the standards, or implementation guides, published by an SDO in this timeframe should include accompanying testing tools.	10. Technology developers, SDOs and government should maintain and update an ongoing suite of testing tools for technology users and developers to support interoperability. 11. ONC and other industry-led certification programs should continue to update certification criteria as needed to support the learning health system's evolving needs.

Category	2015-2017 **Send, receive, find and use priority data elements to improve health and health care quality**	2018-2020 **Expand interoperable health IT and users to improve health and lower cost**	2021-2024 **Achieve nationwide interoperability to enable a learning health system**
	3. Existing industry certification programs should address interoperability functions that ONC's program does not address, in a manner that is complementary to and not duplicative of ONC's certification program, to ensure that different aspects of health IT support a range of interoperability needs. 4. Care providers and professional and trade associations involved in alternative payment models should collect and share ongoing feedback with ONC regarding health IT certification needs for EHRs and other health IT in support of new models of care delivery.	8. Technology developers, SDOs and government should maintain and update an ongoing suite of testing tools for technology users and developers that support interoperability, including tools to test C-CDA, Direct, SOAP and FHIR. 9. ONC and other industry-led certification programs should leverage more stringent testing, including in the field testing, to evaluate interoperability.	12. More than 75% of the test tools approved for use by the ONC Health IT Certification Program should be non-governmental. 13. 100% of the standards, or implementation guides, published by an SDO in this timeframe should include accompanying testing tools.
G3. Commitments	1. ONC will work with NIST and the industry to develop more rigorous testing processes for critical interoperability standards, such as C-CDA. 2. ONC will consider approving non-governmental test tools within its certification program.[96] 3. ONC will make an extensive set of computable data about certified health IT products publicly available on the Certified Health IT Product List (CHPL).	4. ONC, NIST and other health IT stakeholders will provide updated testing tools in support of ONC's Health IT certification program.	5. ONC, NIST and other health IT stakeholders will provide updated testing tools in support of ONC's Health IT certification program.

Table 8. Milestones, Calls to Action and Commitments for Consistent Data Semantics

Category	2015-2017 Send, receive, find and use priority data elements to improve health and health care quality	2018-2020 Expand interoperable health IT and users to improve health and lower cost	2021-2024 Achieve nationwide interoperability to enable a learning health system
H1. Milestones	1. Clinical care providers are able to collect data elements associated with priority data domains once and use them for a variety of purposes, including sharing with individuals, sending during referrals and leveraging for quality measurement.	2. Health-related stakeholders beyond the clinical care delivery system, including researchers, public health, human and community-based services, are able to appropriately access and use relevant data elements associated with priority data domains.	3. A comprehensive testing infrastructure exists for providers to continuously test their health IT as new components are added and old components are phased out to ensure their systems operate as expected after implementation and to hold technology developers and network service providers accountable.
H2. Calls to Action	1. Technology developers should provide accurate translation and adapter services where needed in order to support priority delivery system reform and learning health system needs. 2. Public and private stakeholders should work with SDOs to define a standard approach to federated distribution of centrally maintained code sets, including ongoing support for publicly available, API-enabled repositories like the Value Set Authority Center (VSAC). 3. SDOs should advance and accelerate semantic standards for laboratory orders, other orders and other priorities for a learning health system that require updated or new semantic standards 4. SDOs should advance consumer-friendly terminologies and mappings of accepted synonyms to coded terms.	9. SDOs should develop a process for maintaining compatibility across vocabularies, code sets and value sets in new standards and new versions of existing standards. 10. HHS should provide or endorse mapping and validation tools to help systems ensure data quality across terminologies and ensure compliance with program-related audits.	11. SDOs should follow the developed process for maintaining compatibility across vocabularies, code sets and value sets in new standards and new versions of existing standards.

Category	2015-2017 **Send, receive, find and use priority data elements to improve health and health care quality**	2018-2020 **Expand interoperable health IT and users to improve health and lower cost**	2021-2024 **Achieve nationwide interoperability to enable a learning health system**
	5. Research and clinical trial communities should pilot the use of priority data elements associated with priority data domains for clinical research and precision medicine. 6. Health IT users should provide feedback to SDOs and other stakeholders, including government, regarding additional data elements and/or data domains that should be prioritized for semantic alignment. 7. NLM, FDA, CDC, CMS and other stakeholders should collaborate regarding approaches to promoting laboratory information exchange (especially through the use of LOINC, SNOMED-CT, UCUM and UDIs) between in vitro diagnostic devices and database systems, including laboratory information systems and EHRs. 8 CDC should encourage development of training aids to help laboratories use LOINC for laboratory test ordering and reporting in a structured format that includes data elements necessary to meet CLIA requirements.		
H3. Commitments	1. ONC will promote and participate in collaborative processes to align SDOs and technology developers on the implementation and use of vocabularies, code sets, value sets and structure necessary to consistently represent and maintain the meaning of data elements associated with priority data domains across systems.	2. ONC will continue to promote and participate in collaborative processes to align SDOs and technology developers on the implementation and use of vocabularies, code sets, value sets, and structure necessary to consistently represent and maintain the meaning of priority data elements associated with priority data domains across systems.	Commitments will depend on what the health IT ecosystem needs are as we move towards the 10-year timeframe.

Table 9. Milestones, Calls to Action and Commitments for Consistent Data Formats

Category	2015-2017 Send, receive, find and use priority data elements to improve health and health care quality	2018-2020 Expand interoperable health IT and users to improve health and lower cost	2021-2024 Achieve nationwide interoperability to enable a learning health system
I1. Milestones	1. By the end of 2017, SDOs align semantic standards (vocabulary, code set, value set, and structure where applicable) across electronic health information format standards with semantic standards adopted in ONC's 2015 Edition for priority data domains and associated data elements (see Figure 7 in H. Consistent Data Semantics).	2. By the end of 2020, SDOs agree on semantic standards (vocabulary, code set, value set, and structure where applicable) for priority data domains and associated data elements not defined in ONC's 2015 Edition and align to those standards across electronic health information format standards.	3. As new format standards are developed, SDOs ensure harmony across all format standards, particularly for the priority data domains and associated data elements.
I2. Calls to Action	1. SDOs, in coordination with ONC, should work together to align semantic standards (vocabulary, code set, value set, and structure where applicable) across health information format standards (starting with HL7 v2, C-CDA, QRDA, FHIR, and NCPDP SCRIPT) with semantic standards adopted in ONC's 2015 Edition for priority data domains and associated data elements. 2. Provider and patient-facing technology developers should update their products and services to use format standards identified in ONC's most recent finalized Interoperability Standards Advisory, starting with the most recent version of C-CDA. 3. States and other stakeholders across the ecosystem should further explore and determine the role that NIEM can serve in supporting health information interoperability across domains such as human services and justice.	8. SDOs, in coordination with ONC, should work together to agree on semantic standards (vocabulary, code set, value set, and structure where applicable) for priority data domains and associated data elements not defined in ONC's 2015 Edition and align to those standards across health information format standards. 9. SDOs should develop a process for maintaining compatibility across new format standards and new versions of existing standards. 10. Technology developers should implement updated format standards that reflect aligned semantic standards.	12. Technology developers should continue to implement updated format standards that reflect aligned semantic standards.

Category	2015-2017 **Send, receive, find and use priority data elements to improve health and health care quality**	2018-2020 **Expand interoperable health IT and users to improve health and lower cost**	2021-2024 **Achieve nationwide interoperability to enable a learning health system**
	4. SDOs and stakeholders should document best practices and guidance on methods for exchanging unstructured health information, such as physician notes, in an interoperable manner. 5. Technology developers and providers should use best practices and standardized methods for exchanging unstructured health information, such as physician notes, in an interoperable manner. 6. SDOs and ONC should identify necessary updates to format standards (HL7 v2, C-CDA, QRDA, FHIR and NCPDP) to ensure priority data domains are not only required in those standards, but are also represented consistently across format standards. 7. ONC, NIST, CMS, CDC and FDA should collaborate to advance laboratory data interoperability, including specifications to ensure compliance with CLIA, state and local quality laboratory regulations.	11. Technology developers and SDOs should work together to provide guidance on appropriate rules and testing for generating structured data from native unstructured data.	
I3. Commitments	1. ONC will promote and participate in collaborative processes to align semantic standards across format standards to consistently represent and maintain the meaning of data elements associated with priority data domains across systems.	2. ONC will continue to promote and participate in collaborative processes to align semantic standards across format standards to consistently represent and maintain the meaning of data elements associated with priority data domains across systems.	Commitments will depend on what the health IT ecosystem needs are as we move towards the 10-year timeframe.

Table 10. Milestones, Calls to Action and Commitments for Secure, Standard Services

Category	2015-2017 **Send, receive, find and use priority data elements to improve health and health care quality**	2018-2020 **Expand interoperable health IT and users to improve health and lower cost**	2021-2024 **Achieve nationwide interoperability to enable a learning health system**
J1. Milestones	1. Certification approaches that encourage the adoption of specific APIs or consistently functioning APIs in a manner that does not prevent the adoption of innovative new APIs are developed and implemented by ONC and other industry stakeholders.	2. More than 50% of technology developers provide access to electronic health information through standard, public APIs.	3. More than 75% of technology developers provide access to electronic health information through standard, public APIs.
J2. Calls to Action	1. SDOs, through efforts such as the Data Access Framework (DAF), Argonaut Project and HEART initiative should provide technology developers with profiles, reference implementations, and implementation guides (IGs) to standardize APIs for querying and retrieving priority data elements such as a C-CDA document and as discrete data elements. 2. Technology developers should implement standard APIs from the DAF, HEART and Argonaut projects and make them publicly available. 3. Technology developers should work with SDOs to develop standard APIs for interoperable medical devices. 4. ONC, NIST, CMS, CDC and FDA should collaborate to advance laboratory data interoperability, including the establishment of requirements for common application programming interfaces (APIs) that meet CLIA requirements for laboratory test ordering and reporting.	Calls to action will depend on what the health IT ecosystem needs are as we move towards the six-year timeframe.	Calls to action will depend on what the health IT ecosystem needs are as we move towards the 10-year timeframe.
J3. Commitments	1. ONC will support implementation of new API requirements in certification by working with industry stakeholders to develop and disseminate best practices and technologies to ensure that existing and emerging APIs facilitate interoperability in a secure way.	Commitments will depend on what the health IT ecosystem needs are as we move towards the six-year timeframe.	Commitments will depend on what the health IT ecosystem needs are as we move towards the 10-year timeframe.

Table 11. Milestones, Calls to Action and Commitments for Consistent, Secure Transport Techniques

Category	2015-2017 Send, receive, find and use priority data elements to improve health and health care quality	2018-2020 Expand interoperable health IT and users to improve health and lower cost	2021-2024 Achieve nationwide interoperability to enable a learning health system
K1. Milestones	1. The majority of hospitals, ambulatory providers, and individuals are able to send and receive data elements associated with priority data domains with their trading partners of choice, using at least the Direct transport protocol.	2. Long term care providers and behavioral health providers are able to send and receive data elements associated with priority data domains with their trading partner of choice, using at least the Direct transport protocol.	Calls to action will depend on what the health IT ecosystem needs are as we move towards the 10-year timeframe.
K2. Calls to Action	1. Providers (including hospitals, ambulatory providers, long-term care centers and behavioral health providers) should adopt and use Direct to enable broad scale ability to send and receive data elements associated with priority data domains commensurate with the organization's required LoA. 2. Technology developers and Direct service providers (i.e., HISPs) should join a single common trust community and trust bundle to enable all their users to send and receive priority data elements with each other or develop a simple method for reciprocity between trust communities. 3. Public health agencies should converge on the use of standardized web services to support data submission as well as data query from registries and other systems. 4. Technology developers, providers and research communities should use standards for query functionality identified in ONC's most recent finalized Interoperability Standards Advisory.	Calls to action will depend on what the health IT ecosystem needs are as we move towards the six-year timeframe.	Calls to action will depend on what the health IT ecosystem needs are as we move towards the 10-year timeframe.
K3. Commitments	None at this time.	Commitments will depend on what the health IT ecosystem needs are as we move towards the six-year timeframe.	Commitments will depend on what the health IT ecosystem needs are as we move towards the 10-year timeframe.

Table 12. Milestones, Calls to Action and Commitments for Accurate Individual Data Matching

Category	2015-2017 Send, receive, find and use priority data elements to improve health and health care quality	2018-2020 Expand interoperable health IT and users to improve health and lower cost	2021-2024 Achieve nationwide interoperability to enable a learning health system
L1. Milestones	1. All organizations that match electronic health information have an internal duplicate record rate of no more than 2% at the end of 2017.	2. All organizations that match electronic health information have an internal duplicate record rate of no more than 0.5% at the end of 2020.	3. All organizations that match electronic health information have an internal duplicate record rate of no more than 0.01% at the end of 2024.
L2. Calls to Action	1. Public and private stakeholders should work with SDOs to ensure that data elements for individual data matching are standardized, and can be consistently captured and shared in all health information queries and record linking transactions. 2. The industry should work together to document evidence-based best practices for individual data matching processes, data quality and matching technology. 3. Technology developers and health care organizations, in collaboration with ONC, should advance the use of industry- recognized data definition and data normalization standards.	5. Certified technology developers and data trading partners should consistently include the data elements for individual data matching in exchange transactions. 6. Electronic systems that create individual health records profiles should adopt uniform standards and best practices for capturing and matching health- related data. 7. Health-related organizations should implement a uniform approach to individual data matching and performance measurement that is informed by the best practices documented in L2.2. 8. SDOs and technology developers should advance standards for primary, secondary and voluntary data elements, including the use of unique identifiers and biometrics.	12. Data quality rates in source systems and identity matching services should be within acceptable levels as defined by agreed upon performance metrics. 13. Technology developers should include ubiquitous individual data matching elements in all health IT systems and use improved algorithms to enhance individual data matching accuracy across organizations.

Category	**2015-2017** **Send, receive, find and use priority data elements to improve health and health care quality**	**2018-2020** **Expand interoperable health IT and users to improve health and lower cost**	**2021-2024** **Achieve nationwide interoperability to enable a learning health system**
	4. Technology developers should include the capability to report duplication and matching rates in their products.	9. SDOs should standardize additional, required elements for individual data matching. 10. As new data elements are identified that improve individual data matching, certified health IT developers should include the data elements in health IT systems. 11. SDOs should include matching standards that facilitate interoperability between a broad range of care settings including long term care, infusion centers and mental health facilities.	
L3. Commitments	1. ONC will work with public and private stakeholders to identify and test a core set of metrics that can be used across the health IT ecosystem to consistently assess matching algorithm performance across different data sets and settings.	Commitments will depend on what the health IT ecosystem needs are as we move towards the six-year timeframe.	Commitments will depend on what the health IT ecosystem needs are as we move towards the 10-year timeframe.

Table 13. Milestones, Calls to Action and Commitments for Health Care Directories for Resource Location

Category	2015-2017 Send, receive, find and use priority data elements to improve health and health care quality	2018-2020 Expand interoperable health IT and users to improve health and lower cost	2021-2024 Achieve nationwide interoperability to enable a learning health system
M1. Milestones	1. A glide path for moving from current provider directories to future resource location techniques is developed via a public, transparent process, and widely disseminated.	2. Rules of the road for participating in distributed management of resource location, if appropriate for the architecture and actors, are established via a transparent process. This includes establishing policies and procedures for operation of resource location services, including curation of directory information to maintain data quality.	3. A well-functioning dynamic and distributed architecture for learning health system resource location is in place supported by common national technical standards, and best practices for data quality maintenance and updates.
M2. Calls to Action	1. Provider directory operators should align existing directories to the extent possible with best available standards for provider directories as identified in ONC's most recent finalized Interoperability Standards Advisory or with emerging RESTful approaches if implementation timelines are not near-term. 2. The FACAs should assess the critical health care directory questions identified in the roadmap and how current standards and/or legacy services already incorporated into products can be used or extended to support stakeholder needs. 3. Through public, transparent processes, stakeholders should prioritize the participants and services that are to be discoverable using	5. Through public, transparent processes, stakeholders should identify the architecture and workflow for potential RESTful resource location as part of a learning health system, including the individual and IT system actors, roles and access requirements. 6. Technology developers and resource location service providers should continue to adopt best available national standards for locating participants and resources across the learning health system as identified in ONC's most recent finalized	9. Through public, transparent processes, stakeholders should refine the architecture and workflow for resource location as part of a learning health system.

Category	2015-2017 **Send, receive, find and use priority data elements to improve health and health care quality**	2018-2020 **Expand interoperable health IT and users to improve health and lower cost**	2021-2024 **Achieve nationwide interoperability to enable a learning health system**
	resource location and identify a near-term goal for the first small set of resources to be included in initial implementations, such as Direct addresses, electronic service information, web addresses, and multiple practice locations. 4. CMS should, via various policies, require that Direct addresses and electronic service information are entered into and maintained in NPPES.	Interoperability Standards Advisory. 7. Technology developers and resource location service providers should implement best practices for business processes related to data quality, maintenance and update processes. 8. Through public, transparent processes, stakeholders should work with SDOs and technology developers to demonstrate standard(s) and API(s) for resource location in trial implementations, beginning with a prioritized set of resources.	
M3. Commitments	1. As an interim step, ONC will work with health IT stakeholders to encourage uptake of current provider directory activities. 2. CMS will continue to support efforts to ensure that health plan provider directories are made electronic and published according to best available national standards to support learning health system resource location. 3. ONC and other certification bodies will determine how to support provider directories through certification processes.	Commitments will depend on what the health IT ecosystem needs are as we move towards the six-year timeframe.	Commitments will depend on what the health IT ecosystem needs are as we move towards the 10-year timeframe.

Table 14. Milestones, Calls to Action and Commitments for Individuals Have Access to Longitudinal Electronic Health Information, Can Contribute to that Information, and Can Direct It to Any Electronic Location

Category	2015-2017 Send, receive, find and use priority data elements to improve health and health care quality	2018-2020 Expand interoperable health IT and users to improve health and lower cost	2021-2024 Achieve nationwide interoperability to enable a learning health system
N1. Milestones	1. A majority of individuals are able to securely access their electronic health information and direct it to the destination of their choice.	2. Individuals regularly access and contribute to their longitudinal electronic health information via health IT, send and receive that information through a variety of emerging technologies, and use that information to manage their health and participate in shared-decision making with their care, support and service teams.	3. Individuals are able to seamlessly integrate and compile longitudinal electronic health information across online tools, mobile platforms and devices to participate in shared decision-making with their care, support and service teams.
N2. Calls to Action	1. Health IT purchasers and developers should include individuals and caregivers in the co-creation of digital, accessible health information tools that can securely exchange health information. 2. Health care organizations and consumer groups alike should engage with patients to promote trust that individuals' health information (such as that generated/ collected via home monitoring devices or other emerging technologies) is protected and secure when it is electronically shared. 3. Consumer groups, in collaboration with government agencies, associations and payers should develop and disseminate resources, such as the Blue Button campaign materials,[97] to assist individuals with accessing and using their electronic health information.	5. Individuals and providers should work together to routinely aggregate and reconcile electronic health information from multiple data sources to ensure accuracy and completeness of medical records. 6. Technology developers should deploy innovative, accessible online and mobile platforms/ tools that allow individuals and caregivers to aggregate, reconcile, send, receive and compile information for use in shared decision-making with their care, support and service teams.	7. Individuals and providers should work together to substantially reduce the burden of care coordination through patient-centered tools that aggregate and reconcile electronic health information from across the care continuum and allow for sharing of health information with all care, support and service team members

Category	2015-2017 Send, receive, find and use priority data elements to improve health and health care quality	2018-2020 Expand interoperable health IT and users to improve health and lower cost	2021-2024 Achieve nationwide interoperability to enable a learning health system
	4. Individuals and providers should work together to define a reconciliation process for electronic health information from multiple data sources to ensure accuracy, completeness and a more comprehensive picture of a person.		
N3. Commitments	1. ONC will work with the health IT community to support the Blue Button Initiative to spur consumer demand for their health information and encourage testing and implementation of a portfolio of existing and emerging standards that support consistent methods for sharing health information with individuals. 2. ONC will continue to work with the health IT community to remove barriers and support consumers' ability to access and electronically share their health information with whomever they trust. 3. ONC will promote consistent, easy, and efficient methods for sharing health information with individuals by supporting existing and emerging standards for exchange, including APIs, and continuous iteration and development of those standards in partnership with the health IT community.	4. ONC will work with the health IT community to identify and address additional barriers to nationwide interoperability, including the challenge of consumer access and literacy of their health records.	Commitments will depend on what the health IT ecosystem needs are as we move towards the 10-year timeframe.

Table 15. Milestones, Calls to Action and Commitments for Provider Workflows and Practices Include Consistent Sharing and Use of Patient Information From All Available and Relevant Sources

Category	2015-2017 Send, receive, find and use priority data elements to improve health and health care quality	2018-2020 Expand interoperable health IT and users to improve health and lower cost	2021-2024 Achieve nationwide interoperability to enable a learning health system
O1. Milestones	1. Providers evolve care processes and information reconciliation to ensure essential health information is sent, found and/or received to support safe transitions in care.	2. Providers routinely and proactively seek outside information about individuals and can use it to coordinate care.	3. Providers routinely use relevant info from a variety of sources, including environmental, occupational, genetic, human service and cutting edge research evidence to tailor care to the individual.
O2. Calls to Action	1. Technology developers should develop technology platforms that allow providers and other users to perform certain key interoperability functions, such as standardized exchange, within their system with minimal effort and ease, using clear instructions provided by the technology developers and made publicly available. 2. Providers and their staff should proactively offer individuals timely electronic access to their own health information and encourage them to access it. 3. Providers should use the "Blue Button" and the Blue Button® and Download My Data® marks to indicate where consumers can go online to access their health information 4. Public and private stakeholders should incorporate interoperability into the training of new providers and continuing professional education.	5. Providers should support the incorporation of patient-generated health data in health care delivery and research and incorporate such data as appropriate. 6. Public and private stakeholders should agree on a way in which to evaluate the progress and competency of trainees to find, send, receive and use relevant information to coordinate an individual's care.	7. Providers should leverage a robust library of interoperable workflows to support care processes across the continuum of care, including tools for integration, reconciliation and validation of external information. 8. Initial and ongoing training for providers should be fully integrated into the learning health system so that real time analytics, benchmarking and feedback are used for care delivery, care improvement and provider maintenance of certification. 9. Providers should use new evidence-based guidelines and tools for care that are disseminated rapidly to providers through clinical decision support and other timely and context-sensitive pathways.

Category	2015-2017 **Send, receive, find and use priority data elements to improve health and health care quality**	2018-2020 **Expand interoperable health IT and users to improve health and lower cost**	2021-2024 **Achieve nationwide interoperability to enable a learning health system**
O3. Commitments	1. ONC, federal agencies and the industry will identify additional best practices for the incorporation of patient-generated health data in health care delivery and research. 2. ONC will develop a Health IT Playbook consisting of tools and resources designed to assist providers working towards the adoption and optimization of health IT, including key interoperability workflow considerations, and engaging consumers to access and use their electronic health information.	Commitments will depend on what the health IT ecosystem needs are as we move towards the six-year timeframe.	Commitments will depend on what the health IT ecosystem needs are as we move towards the 10-year timeframe.

Table 16. Milestones, Calls to Action and Commitments for Measuring Success

Category	2015-2017 **Send, receive, find and use priority data elements to improve health and health care quality**	2018-2020	2021-2024
P1. Milestones	1. ONC, federal partners and stakeholders develop a set of measures assessing interoperable exchange and the impact of interoperability on key processes that enable improved health and health care.	2. Public and private stakeholders report on progress towards interoperable exchange; including identifying barriers to interoperability, lessons learned and impacts of interoperability on health outcomes and costs.	3. Public and private stakeholders report on progress on key metrics identified to achieve a learning health system.
P2. Calls to Action	1. Industry and health care organizations that enable exchange (e.g. HISPS, HIOs) should provide input on how to address	6. Public and private stakeholders should publicly report on	Calls to action will depend on what the health IT ecosystem

Table 16. (Continued)

Category	2015-2017 Send, receive, find and use priority data elements to improve health and health care quality	2018-2020	2021-2024
	measurement needs including identifying ways to address measurement gaps using data generated by systems and infrastructure that enables interoperable exchange. 2. The behavioral health community should work with ONC and federal partners such as SAMHSA to determine the community's health IT needs and ways to measure interoperable exchange among their providers. 3. The LTPAC community should work with ONC and federal partners such as CMS to determine the community's health IT needs and ways to measure interoperable exchange among their providers. 4. Stakeholders, federal partners, and ONC should work together to identify measures related to individuals and determine ways to address measurement gaps (i.e., consumer engagement in measurement, use of patient-generated health data.) 5. Stakeholders across the broader ecosystem (i.e., non-health settings) should work with ONC and federal partners to identify measures and potential data sources across their respective communities.	progress made on (1) measures identified during the three-year agenda of the Roadmap; and (2) progress made in achieving milestones identified in the Roadmap. 7. External stakeholders critical to supporting a learning health system (e.g. ACOs, research consortia) should work with ONC and other federal partners to identify key metrics and address measurement gaps.	needs are as we move towards the 10-year timeframe.
P3. Commitments	1. ONC will analyze and report on nationwide progress, including a report to Congress on proposed measures mandated under MACRA.[98] 2. ONC will work with federal partners and stakeholders to address measurement gaps, and identify future measures resulting in the development of a long-term measurement framework. This includes consulting with external	3. ONC will continue to update the measurement framework according to the needs of the health IT landscape and report on nationwide progress. This will include reporting to Congress on progress related to interoperability	5. ONC will continue to update the measurement framework according to the needs of the health IT landscape and report on nationwide progress.

Category	2015-2017 **Send, receive, find and use priority data elements to improve health and health care quality**	2018-2020	2021-2024
	stakeholders to develop proposed measures as mandated under MACRA.[99]	as mandated under MACRA.[100] 4. ONC will work with federal partners to incorporate measurement of settings beyond healthcare and outcomes of interoperability.	6. ONC will work with federal partners and other stakeholders to incorporate measurement of learning health systems.

End Notes

[1] http:// www.healthit.gov/ sites/default/files/ ONC10yearInteroperability ConceptPaper.pdf

[2] http://www.ieee.org/educationcareers/education/standards/standards glossary. html

[3] http:// www.healthit.gov/ sites/default/files/ ONC10yearInteroperability ConceptPaper.pdf

[4] Medicare Access and CHIP Reauthorization Act of 2015 (MACRA) (P.L. 114-10 Sec 106)

[5] http://www.healthit.gov/policy-researchers-implementers/health-it-strategic-planning

[6] Charles D, Swain M Patel V. (July 2015) Interoperability among U.S. Non-federal Acute Care Hospitals. ONC Data Brief, no.28. Office of the National Coordinator for Health Information Technology: Washington DC.

[7] Despite Substantial Progress in EHR Adoption, Health Information Exchange and Patient Engagement Remain Low In Office Settings. Michael F. Furukawa, Jennifer King, Vaishali Patel, Chun-Ju Hsiao, Julia Adler-Milstein and Ashish K. Jha. Health Affairs, 33, no.9 (2014):1672-1679. 10.1377/hlthaff.2014.0445

[8] Derived from the Institute of Electrical and Electronics Engineers (IEEE) definition of interoperability. http:// www.ieee.org/ educationcareers/ education/ standards/ standards glossary.html

[9] Administrative data includes data related to payment, eligibility and benefits.

[10] http:// www.healthit.gov/ sites/default/files/ ONC10yearInteroperability ConceptPaper.pdf

[11] Many care settings and care providers are not eligible for the Medicare and Medicaid EHR Incentive Programs

[12] See http:// healthit.gov/ sites/default/ files/acceleratinghieprinciples _ strategy.pdf

[13] http://www.hhs.gov/blog/2015/01/26/progress-towards-better-care-smarter-spending-healthier-people.html

[14] http://innovation.cms.gov/

[15] Note that technology is not stationary either.

[16] http://www.commonwellalliance.org/about/

[17] http://sequoiaproject.org/carequality/what-we-do/

[18] http://sequoiaproject.org/ehealth-exchange/

[19] http://www.directtrust.org/about-us/

[20] As an example, the Data Use and Reciprocal Support Agreement (DURSA) is a single, multi-party agreement that sets the rules by which participants operate to exchange data. It is used today primarily by the Sequoia Project for participation in the eHealth Exchange network.

[21] As an example, DirectTrust works with the Electronic Healthcare Network Accreditation Commission to independently accredit HISPs as Direct Trusted Agents.

[22] Interoperability Workgroup Governance Subgroup Presentation. July 2014. https:// www. healthit.gov/ facas/calendar/2014/07/23/policy- governance-subgroup

[23] As a federal advisory committee focused on accelerating the development and adoption of health information technology and the Nationwide Health Information Network (NwHIN), AHIC worked with organizations like the Markle Foundation to develop principles and frameworks for health information exchange, none of which required adoption or participation by organizations participating in health information exchange.

[24] American Recovery and Reinvestment Act of 2009. 111th Congress. January 2009. http:// www.gpo.gov/fdsys/ pkg/ BILLS-111hr1enr/pdf/BILLS-111hr1enr. pdf

[25] Section 3001(c)(8) of the Public Health Service Act, HITECH SEC. 3001. Office of the National Coordinator for Health IT. (8) Governance for Nationwide Health Information Network.—The National Coordinator shall establish a governance mechanism for the nationwide health information network.42 U.S.C. § 300jj-11.

[26] The RFI sought public comment on a regulatory approach to establish a governance mechanism that would create conditions for trusted exchange amongst all of these organizations and set the rules of the road for exchange.

[27] http://www.healthit.gov/sites/default/files/GovernanceFrameworkTrustedEHIE Final.pdf

[28] http://www.healthit.gov/sites/default/files/wscfinalreport.pdf

[29] http://www.healthit.gov/policy-researchers-implementers/exemplar-hie-governance-entities-program

[30] The priority data domains are clinical to begin with, but should expand over time to cover many other types of information, including social determinants of health.

[31] https:// www.whitehouse.gov/ the-press-office/ 2015/ 02/ 13/ fact-sheet-white-house-summit-cybersecurity-and-consumer-protection

[32] US cybercrime: Rising risks, reduced readiness Key findings from the 2014 US State of Cybercrime Survey. PWC. June 2014. http:// www.pwc.com/ en_US/ us/ increasing-it-effectiveness/ publications/assets/pwc-2014-us-state-of-cybercrime.pdf

[33] http:// www.illuminweb.com/ wp-content/ uploads/ ill-mo-uploads/ 103/ 2418/ health-systems-cyber-intrusions.pdf

[34] NIST Special Publication 800-57.

[35] 45 CFR § 164.404(a)

[36] 45 CFR §§ 164.400-414

[37] https://buildsecurityin.us-cert.gov/

[38] http://www.nist.gov/itl/csd/sp800-160-051314.cfm

[39] 45 CFR § 164.312(d)

[40] http://www.nist.gov/nstic/index.html

[41] NSTIC Proposers Conference. Jeremy Grant, NIST. February 2012. http:// pptfilesearch.com/ single/655550/nstic-proposers-conference-15-february-2012

[42] http://www.nist.gov/nstic/privacy-workshop-presentations.html

[43] Improving the Security of Consumer Financial Transactions. October 17, 2014. http:// www. whitehouse.gov/the-press-office/2014/10/17/executive-order-improving-security-consumer-financial-transactions

[44] Note that electronic health information exchange with federal agencies often requires even higher levels of assurance. For example, the Department of Defense requires LOA 4.

[45] http:// www.healthit.gov/ facas/ health-it-policy-committee/ health-it-policy-committee-recommendations-national-coordinator-health-it

[46] The Internet of Things (IoT) refers to the connection of a wide variety of uniquely identifiable devices across the existing Internet infrastructure (e.g., smart phones, wearable and implantable devices, etc.).

[47] http://www.consumer.ftc.gov/articles/0171-medical-identity-theft

[48] http://www.va.gov/identitytheft/

[49] 45 CFR § 164.508

[50] 45 CFR § 164.506

[51] Electronic Consent Management Final Report, October 2014, http:// www.healthit.gov/ sites/ default/files/privacy-security/ecm_finalreport_forrelease62415.pdf

[52] 45 CFR § 164.524

[53] 45 CFR § 164.506

[54] http://www.justice.gov/opcl/docs/rec-com-rights.pdf. In 1973, the Department of Health, Education, and Welfare (HEW) released its report, Records, Computers, and the Rights of Citizens, which outlined a Code of Fair Information Practices that would create "safeguard requirements" for certain "automated personal data systems" maintained by the Federal Government. This Code of Fair Information Practices is now commonly referred to as fair information practice principles (FIPPs).

[55] 45 CFR § 164.520. For model Notices of Privacy Practices: http://www.healthit.gov/providers-professionals/model-notices-privacy-practices.

[56] 42 USC § 290dd-2; See http://www.ecfr.gov/cgi-bin/text-idx?c=ecfr&sid= 02b3d31742318b 503b8d4ba0111d0e35&tpl=/ecfrbrowse/ Title42/42cfr2_main_02.tpl

[57] 42 USC § 290dd-2

[58] 38 USC § 7332, See http:// www.gpo.gov/ fdsys/ pkg/ USCODE-2011-title38/ pdf/ USCODE-2011-title38-partV-chap73-subchapIII-sec7332.pdf

[59] Electronic Consent Management Final Report, October 2014, http:// www.healthit.gov/ sites/ default/files/privacy-security/ecm_finalreport_ forrelease62415.pdf

[60] The ability of an electronic health information system to capture, adjudicate, comply with and persist in downstream processing of the information an individual's documented choice (basic or granular) about whether information about them should be available for electronic exchange within the learning health system. See Appendix B of the Supplemental Materials.

[61] http:// www.healthit.gov/ facas/ calendar/ 2014/12/17/ standards-transport-security-standards-workgroup

[62] Basic Choice is the choice offered to an individual to prevent his/her PHI from being available for electronic exchange when it otherwise would be for purposes of TPO (without an individual's permission) because it is allowed by the HIPAA Privacy Rule, and no other laws requiring permission such as 42 CFR Part 2, or state enacted laws, apply. Granular Choice is the choice an individual makes regarding the distinctions between legally sensitive clinical conditions, such as mental health or HIV/AIDS status and evolves over time to enable choice about disclosure to specifically identified participants in the health care system.

[63] The ability of an electronic health information system to capture, adjudicate, comply with and persist in downstream processing of the information an individual's documented choice (basic or granular) about whether information about them should be available for electronic exchange within the learning health system. See Appendix B in the Supplemental Materials document.

[64] Section 3001(c)(5) of the PHSA provides the National Coordinator with the authority to establish a certification program or programs for the voluntary certification of health IT. Specifically, section 3001(c)(5)(A) specifies that the "National Coordinator, in consultation with the Director of the National Institute of Standards and Technology, shall keep or recognize a program or programs for the voluntary certification of health information technology as being in compliance with applicable certification criteria adopted under this subtitle" (i.e., certification criteria adopted by the Secretary under section 3004 of the PHSA).

[65] 45 CFR §170.315

[66] http://www.hl7.org/implement/standards/fhir/summary.html

[67] 145 CFR § 170.315

[68] https://www.niem.gov/technical/Pages/The-Model.aspx

[69] 45 CFR § 170.315

[70] Core Measure 8 (eligible professionals) and Core Measure 12 (eligible hospitals). 42 CFR Parts 412, 413, and 495. Medicare and Medicaid Programs; the Medicare and Medicaid EHR Incentive Program--Stage 2. September 2012. http://www.gpo.gov/fdsys/pkg/FR-2012-09-04/pdf/2012-21050.pdf

[71] The April 2014 JASON Report, A Robust Health Data Structure, recommended that, "interoperability issues can be resolved only by establishing a comprehensive, transparent and overarching software architecture for health information." The report further defines architecture as "the collective components of a software system that interact in specified ways and across specified interfaces to ensure specified functionality." In this context, the report goes on to call for standards, interfaces and protocols that are open and APIs that are public. Following the JASON Report, the HIT Policy Committee convened a task force to review the report's recommendations and subsequently advise ONC on the adoption of the report's recommendations. The task force called for a coordinated architecture that, rather than being top- down in nature, would be more loosely coupled, enabled by public APIs defined by the group as uniformly available, non-proprietary, tested by a trusted third party and operating within well-define business and legal frameworks. Report available at: http:// healthit.gov/ sites/ default/files/ptp13-700hhs_white.pdf

[72] Ibid.

[73] One example of such an implementation is the Federal Health Architecture's SOAP-based CONNECT Software that is used by many participants in the eHealth Exchange.

[74] Public Law 105–277. 105th Congress. October 21, 1998. http:// www.gpo.gov/ fdsys/ pkg/ PLAW-105publ277/pdf/PLAW-105publ277.pdf

[75] Patient Identification and Matching Final Report. Prepared for the Office of the National Coordinator by Audacious Inquiry. February 2014. https:// www.healthit.gov/ sites/ default/ files/patient_identification_matching_final_report.pdf

[76] The nature and occurrence of registration errors in the emergency department. AF Hakimzada, RA Green, OR Sayan et al. Int J Med Inform. 2008; 77:169-175. http:// www.ncbi.nlm.nih.gov/ pubmed/17560165

[77] http://perspectives.ahima.org/patient-matching-in-health. VVTK 4u 8cTcs

[78] Patient Identification and Matching Final Report. Prepared for the Office of the National Coordinator by Audacious Inquiry. February 2014. https:// www.healthit.gov/ sites/ default/ files/patient identification matching final report.pdf

[79] http://www.healthit.gov/safer/guide/sg006

[80] MPI Clean-up: It's a Must. AHIMA Webinar. July 2009. http:// campus.ahima.org/ audio/ 2009/RB072109.pdf

[81] http://surescripts.com/news-center/national-progress-report-2014

[82] NPPES is the National Enumeration System responsible for assigning the National Provider Identifier (NPI) as mandated by HIPAA. The NPI is a 10-digit unique identifier, similar to a SSN or Corporate Tax Number, used in most health care related transactions such as: enrollment with government and private payers, claims payment, prescriptions and health records management. Currently over 4.2 million NPIs have been assigned to health care individuals and organizations.

[83] The use of the NPPES database has increased over time. On average more than 2,000 users download the publicly available file each month and over 25,000 new NPIs are registered each month.

[84] http:// www.hhs.gov/ idealab/ projects-item/ modernizing-the-national-plan-and-provider-enumeration-system/

[85] 45 CFR § 164.524

[86] Individuals' Access and Use of their Online Medical Record Nationwide: ONC Data Brief #20. September 2014. http:// www.healthit.gov/ sites/default/files/ consumeraccessdatabrief _9_10_14.pdf

[87] See the Supplemental Materials document for more information about each initiative.

[88] http://www.healthit.gov/policy-researchers-implementers/person-center

[89] http://www.medicaid.gov/medicaid-chip-program-information/by-topics/long-term-services-and-supports/downloads/ltss-expenditures-fy2013.pdf

[90] For purposes of this Roadmap, the term "providers" is broadly inclusive of the care continuum and includes individuals and organizations that hold professional licenses and certifications that grant them permission to play a role in the treatment of individuals as part of a community. This includes providers such as primary care physicians, specialists, nurses, physical therapists, pharmacists, dentists, social workers, optometrists and other allied health professionals, as well as organizations such as hospitals, public health departments, mental health and substance use disorder treatment services, long- term and post-acute care facilities, home and community-based services, other support service providers, care managers and other authorized individuals and institutions.

[91] For more information, see Sec 101(e) of the 2015 Medicare and CHIP Reauthorization Act.

[92] Ibid

[93] The Cybersecurity Framework (http://www.nist.gov/cyberframework/index.cfm) provides a common language and systematic methodology for managing cyber risk and can be used to help identify and prioritize actions for reducing risk. It enables organizations—regardless of size, degree of cybersecurity risk, or cybersecurity sophistication—to apply the principles and best practices of risk management to make critical infrastructure more secure. It is also

flexible by design and allows organizations, including those within the Health and Public Health (HPH) Sector, to apply the Framework in their own context.

[94] http://csrc.nist.gov/publications/fips/fips140-2/fips1402annexa.pdf

[95] See the Supplemental Materials Document for a detailed discussion on Basic and Granular Choice.

[96] See https://www.federalregister.gov/articles/2015/06/09/2015-13510/acceptance-and-approval-of-non-governmental-developed-test-procedures-test-tools-and-test-data-for

[97] http://www.healthit.gov/patients-families/blue-button-psa-campaign

[98] P.L. 114-10 §106

[99] Ibid.

[100] Ibid.

INDEX

T

V

W

X